THE PROSPECTS OF HUMANISM

THE PROSPECTS OF HUMANISM

BY

LAWRENCE HYDE

Author of *The Learned Knife*

GREENWOOD PRESS, PUBLISHERS

WESTPORT, CONNECTICUT

Originally published in 1931
by Charles Scribner's Sons

First Greenwood Reprinting 1970

SBN 8371-2966-4

PRINTED IN UNITED STATES OF AMERICA

To

W. Y. E.

We cannot but look up with reverence to the advanced natures of the naturalists and moralists in highest repute amongst us, and wish they had been heightened by a more noble principle, which had crowned all their various sciences with the principal science, and in their brave strayings after truth helped them to better fortune than only to meet with her handmaids, and kept them from the fate of Ulysses, who wandering through the shades met all the ghosts, yet could not see the queen.

J. H. his Motion to the Parliament of England concerning the Advancement of Learning, quoted by Coleridge in *The Friend*

CONTENTS

THE PROSPECTS OF HUMANISM

CHAPTER I

INTRODUCTORY

THE last century was very definitely preoccupied with institutions, with the external conditions of existence, with problems of political and social freedom. It was an age of Liberalism, an age in which men's minds were concerned to an outstanding degree with the task of emancipating humanity from limitations which were imposed upon it from without. Its keynote was a resolute affirmation of the principle of Individualism.

Today the aims which the Victorians set themselves have in a large measure been attained. So far at least as the English-speaking populations of the world are concerned the democratic ideal may be said to have been substantially realized. Woman has at last secured for herself an equality with man. The constitution of the modern state leaves us all free to trade, worship God, give expression to our convictions, educate our children as we think fit. In this particular direction there is, comparatively speaking, little that remains to be done. We have entered in a very complete fashion into our twentieth-century heritage.

There is, however, another side to this achievement. It is becoming more and more evident that the Victorians in solving their problems have only presented us with another of even more formidable dimensions: that of preventing the emancipated modern from exercising his newly acquired liberty in a destructive, wasteful, and ignoble fashion. The task before us is that of persuading a race of beings who are to an exceptional degree free from external restraints, to impose some sort of voluntary restraint upon themselves. Everybody is able today to 'do as he likes', but what he likes to do is only too frequently something ugly, crude, banal, or positively subversive. The finer values of civilization are slowly but surely being destroyed. A great wave of vulgarization is sweeping over the world. Everything tends to be dragged down to the level on which it is comprehensible or emotionally satisfying to the man who has neither purified his perceptions, disciplined his will, nor cultivated his mind. From one point of view at least the fruit of Liberalism is libertinism.

It is largely because they are so acutely conscious of the seriousness of this threat to culture that recent critics are to be distinguished from their predecessors of the period preceding the War. Their interest is very definitely psychological rather than social or political. Realizing that the basis of all external forms is in the last resort the integrity of the individual, they are engaged in exploring in a remarkably searching fashion the spiritual, instead of the material, foundations of our distracted modern civilization.

Now the distinctive note of the dominant nineteenth-century philosophy was the emphasis which it laid upon the place of man in the biological scheme. He was regarded as an animal of exceptional intelligence, the inner principle of whose life was essentially similar to that of all the other inhabitants of the planet, and who had it in his power, by a combination of patience and scientific knowledge, to transform the world into an agreeable and habitable place. Most important of all, he was by nature good rather than bad; in so far as he was corrupted it was through his external circumstances. Modify his environment and his shortcomings would speedily disappear.

The accepted modern designation of this attitude is that of Humanitarianism. That, on the contrary, by which it is today being disputed is properly described as Humanism, and it is distinguished by the fact that it lays stress before everything upon the *opposition* between Man and Nature. According to this view, although Man is indisputably a part of Nature, he has also within him something which is different from the natural; he is that in which the natural and something other than the natural are united. And this fact finds its characteristic expression in our experience of free-will, and particularly in our power, shared by no other animal, of imposing a veto upon our expansive instinctive desires.

It is the belief of the modern humanist that the disorders in which we are at present so disastrously implicated will never be resolved until men again come to realize and express the fact of their distinctive humanity. And this is equivalent to saying that the real problem before us is that of achieving disciplined individuality. We must control ourselves before we can effectively control our environment. And we can only exercise that control from a centre which is established above the plane of the flux.*

Those who are contending against the naturalism of the humanitarians are, however, by no means united amongst themselves. To the attitude of the classical humanists there is sharply opposed that of the neo-romantics, represented in England most characteristically by Mr J. Middleton Murry and Mr Hugh I'A. Fausset. These writers reject the humanistic view on the ground that it leaves us in the end with an unresolved dualism. They contend that the obligation upon us is that of achieving a radical synthesis between the discordant elements in our being, as a result of which the tension between the instincts and the ethical will is completely overcome. We must pass beyond the plane of the moral; the 'New Man' must be born within us.

* The reader will find this point of view expounded with exceptional lucidity and power in Mr F. McEachran's *The Civilized Man* (1930).

The standpoint of the romantic presents us with a curious problem. For, on the one hand, he is uncompromisingly 'naturalistic' in his outlook, rejecting completely the notion of man's being different in essence from other forms of biological life. And yet, on the other, his attitude is clearly distinguished from that of the humanitarian, since, like the classical humanist, he concentrates his attention upon the re-creation of the individual. He may be said, therefore, to belong in a very definite fashion to the new school of criticism rather than to the old.

In addition to those critics who are in a clear-cut sense either 'classical' or 'romantic' in tendency, we have to take account of numbers of others who are resolute in their repudiation of the values of the 'humanitarian' thinker. In fact, it is not too much to say that there is scarcely a critic of any distinction among us today who is not, in one way or another, concerned with the fundamental problem of the transmutation of the self. We are, it would seem, confronted with a definitely new orientation of thought. Writers like Mr Shaw and Mr Wells, with their almost exclusive preoccupation with the more external features of the social problem, have now ceased to exert any really significant influence upon the modern mind. Our attention is being increasingly directed to those more radical psychological issues which the men of their time never properly brought themselves to face. We are approaching the question from a diametrically opposite direction.

Thus, to mention only some of the more outstanding names, we have in France Julien Benda and Ramon Fernandez, in Germany the late Walther Rathenau, Count Keyserling, and Robert Curtius. In America we have the 'new humanists', with Irving Babbitt and Paul Elmer More at their head, and such men as Walter Lippmann, Joseph Wood Krutch, Waldo Frank, Allen Tate, and Montgomery Belgion; in England the late T. E. Hulme,

General Smuts, Wyndham Lewis, T. S. Eliot, Herbert Read, F. McEachran, C. E. M. Joad, Middleton Murry, H. I'A. Fausset, and Adrian Stokes. All these men are serious writers, the majority of them of established reputation. And, diverse as are their points of view in regard to many issues, they may yet all be said to be fighting on the same front. They are in process of recoil from the superficial and unjustified optimism of the last century. They are all conscious of the fact that the 'emancipated' man of today has become enslaved by certain ignoble inclinations which he can only overcome by some form of discipline imposed upon himself from within. They are all concerned with getting down to fundamental principles of philosophical criticism. And they are all profoundly dissatisfied with existing standards of value.

It is impossible, however, to read these critics without being struck by a fact of singular significance: their philosophical basis is definitely humanistic rather than religious. With rare exceptions they are men whose attitude is essentially secular. There are those among them, certainly, like Mr More and Mr Eliot, who avowedly take their stand upon the principles of religion. But it can hardly be said that their faith is of a very forceful kind. The exact nature of the 'religion' by which Mr More is inspired still remains somewhat obscure, as do also the respects in which his standpoint differs from that of the 'pure' humanist. Mr Eliot has done some valuable work in pointing out the limitations of the humanistic attitude, but his recent conversion to Anglo-Catholicism scarcely seems to have brought with it as yet any notable deepening of vision or insight; it is still primarily as a distinguished philosophical critic that he is today a force among us. As for those who, like Mr Lippmann, are impressing upon us the value of the teachings of 'high religion', it is plain that such doctrines as they respond to are either in themselves more philosophical than religious, or become such in the process of being commended to our attention.*

When we turn to the 'new romantics' we are met, it is true, with a somewhat different state of affairs. From one point of view their outlook may reasonably be described as 'religious'. For they are indisputably living on the religious plane, in the sense that they are preoccupied with such problems as those of the transmutation of the lower nature, union with the Whole, and the validation of the data of 'intuition'. And it is plain also that the romantic faith can make in practice for very much the same type of behaviour as that which results from sincere religious belief. It may not be too much to say that the finest type of romantic is a religionist who for one reason or another hesitates to admit the real nature of his inspiration, or who has made an imperfect analysis of his experience.

We must not forget, however, that between implicit and explicit religion there is a significant difference. The fact remains that with his conscious mind the modern romantic decisively rejects the religious conception of the universe. He is a determined opponent of anything in the nature of transcendentalism or supernaturalism. For Mr Murry, who is the most important representative of this tendency in England, there is no God, nor any need to postulate His existence.

In view of these considerations I think I am justified, for the purpose of this essay, in describing the modern critical movement, both in its classical and its romantic

* Thus Mr Eliot writes of Mr Babbitt: 'I should say that he regarded Confucius, Buddha, Socrates, and Erasmus as humanists. . . . It may surprise some to see Confucius and Buddha, who are popularly regarded as founders of religions, in this list. But it is always the human reason, not the revelation of the supernatural, upon which Mr Babbitt insists'. (*For Lancelot Andrewes*, p. 131)

aspects, as being definitely 'humanistic' in tendency. The values of these writers may possibly from one point of view be regarded as religious, but they are certainly not religious in the sense that those of even the most extreme type of modernist churchman are. The consciousness out of which they are writing cannot be fairly identified with the religious consciousness. They do not find in the fact of God a centre to which all their thinking must be related. Their trust is essentially in man's native powers. Some of them may, indeed, believe that man is something more than a part of Nature, but the fact remains that they conceive of him as capable of ordering his affairs without consciously looking upward to a suprahuman region of being for inspiration.

What, then, is the exact nature of the alternative to which they are as a consequence committed? The question is one to which it is by no means easy to give a clear and satisfactory answer—as the exponents of modern Humanism are beginning to discover to their cost. But we are safe, I think, in assuming that Humanism entails a reliance upon the operation of three cultural agencies: rational, ethical, and æsthetic respectively. If somehow or other people can be induced to exercise their reason in a proper fashion, to respect the moral law, and to respond to the elevating influence of art, then we may perhaps one day enjoy the privilege of living in a harmonious and stable type of society. If they cannot be so induced, then we are lost. For there is nothing left on which we are able to depend.

The distinctive character of the religious attitude, on the contrary, lies in the individual's profound realization of his dependence upon a Higher Power. He regards himself as creative only in so far as he contrives to associate himself with a source of enlightenment and strength which he conceives as lying beyond the human plane. His faith is not in Man, but in Man in union with God.

He believes certainly that man must save himself by the exercise of his natural faculties, but he regards those faculties as inadequate unless they are quickened and fortified as a result of his contact with the Divine.

Hence, when he is confronted with the standpoint of the humanist he will immediately question whether we can afford to rely upon these three cultural agencies *by themselves*. He will recognize, of course, that the eventual spiritualizing of man and society must necessarily be accomplished through the threefold mode of the rational, the moral, and the æsthetic; what alternative, indeed, could possibly exist? But he will express his doubts as to how far preoccupation with reason, ethics, and art will by itself enable us to redeem society. He will maintain that man's capacity to order his existence in accordance with the principles of truth, goodness, and beauty is determined in the last resort by his initial success in relating himself to That in which they have their source.

But I am well aware that to treat the problem of Humanism from this point of view would be a profitless proceeding. Conviction in a matter of this order cannot be the fruit of argument and disputation; the decisive factor can only be a profound type of interior experience. For this reason I have undertaken nothing in the nature of a direct apology for Religion, even as thus broadly conceived. I have chosen, rather, to concentrate primarily upon the ideas and theories which are put forward by our modern humanistic philosophers and to enquire how far they would appear to take us. Hence, although it would be idle to pretend that the object of this study is not that of advancing a plea for Religion, it remains true that that plea is made more by implication than otherwise. My primary concern has been to show that in the end the purely humanistic attitude to the world breaks down, and that in so breaking down it points beyond itself to the superior validity of the religious experience.

As to the plan of the work, I have considered in turn our relationship to the True, the Good, and the Beautiful, and tried to indicate as clearly as possible how unsatisfactory that relationship remains until the consciousness has become deepened as a result of some type of religious illumination. This has involved an examination at the appropriate points of the 'classical' and the 'romantic' attitudes to life. But the book is not by any means concerned exclusively with philosophical theories. Included in its scope is a study of the psychology of the man of today who is consciously or unconsciously attempting to live his life on 'humanistic' principles, attempting to dispense with any definite religious belief.

Finally, I have not hesitated to examine in some detail theories and standpoints which are more particular to individuals than broadly representative of given schools of thought. For the influence of certain ideas today in this field is closely associated in the minds of the majority with those personalities by whom they have been most persuasively presented. Hence it becomes almost incumbent upon the critic to consider the attitude of such personalities in relation to somewhat wider issues, in order that those of their theories which are directly in question may, as it were, to some degree be evaluated by implication. But I believe that what appear to be of the nature of divagations will be found in the end to reinforce the argument which it is the purpose of this essay to advance.

CHAPTER II

THOUGHT AND BEING

In concluding the preceding chapter I made it clear that the claim which I am advancing in this essay for the values of religion is of a strictly limited type. I am concerned only to support the contention that man cannot effectively solve his problems unless he is prepared to look upwards for inspiration to something which lies above the plane of the purely human. Hence in considering here the relationship between our intellectual processes and our inward condition of being I shall do no more than attempt to show that the more ultimate truths about ourselves and the world disclose themselves only to those who are not merely intelligent, but spiritually quickened as well. And this, again, is equivalent to saying that when we become engaged with the more fundamental issues in life the intellect begins to fail us unless it has been co-ordinated with the heart; understanding becomes as much a matter of love as of intellectual penetration. The thesis is one which is defended with singular skill and persuasiveness by our modern romantic philosophers, who in this matter may be said to see eye to eye with the more orthodox religious thinker.

1. Passion and Vision

Thought is a function of being: the head follows the heart. We meet here with an important principle, but one which at the same time lends itself all too readily to serious misinterpretation.

It is fashionable at the present time to emphasize the derivative character of our rational processes. A great part of our mental energies are, it is alleged, devoted to 'rationalizing' our unconscious prejudices. The conclusions to which our analyses lead us have been predetermined before we sat down to think. Our reason is most of the time playing the part of an accessory after the act. So our modern psychologists are at great pains to point out to us by elaborate arguments which, we are to assume, are themselves to be regarded as exempt from the general rule that all demonstrations are suspect.

That we do nevertheless owe to their researches a deepened insight into the way in which our syllogisms bend to our desires is evident enough. But this is not to say that we need be driven as a result to embrace that shallow and cynical philosophy of subjectivism which finds such wide acceptance among the more educated today. For there is another side to the question which we cannot afford to leave out of account.

When there is an alteration in the tensions existing in the depth of a man's subconscious self, his philosophy becomes modified; willy-nilly he finds himself inhabiting a new world, looking upon life with a different eye. For his taste in speculative ideas, like his taste in amusements, literature, and women, is determined primarily by his inner condition of being. When that changes his predilections change too. So from this point of view it is not inaccurate to say that his vision is subjectively conditioned.

But we are not therefore entitled to conclude that the changing aspects of the universe in which he lives are nothing more than emanations of his changing self. It is equally valid to assume that the alteration in his internal condition has rendered it possible for him to apprehend for the first time objects which have always been in existence outside himself, merely waiting to be perceived. In order to appreciate the force of certain intellectual considerations it is necessary first of all to have the attention inclined in a particular direction, just as it is necessary to tune-in one's wireless set in order to receive on a given wave-length. A ship on the horizon does not only come into existence at the moment when I focus my vision upon it. Nor is the existence of God invalidated because it only becomes apparent to those who have first purified their natures.

Metaphysically speaking, the most that we can say of the pink snakes which insinuate themselves into the dipsomaniac's field of vision is that they exist in another dimension from that of the chairs and tables in the room. To describe that dimension as 'subjective' is merely to evade the issue. All that we are permitted to observe is that the condition for entering the world in which such snakes appear is a certain state of psychological adjustment (or, if you will, maladjustment). But this applies equally to the world of the saint, the artist, and the man in the street. 'That which appears to each, is'.*

The more penetrating the understanding, the more vital the categories with which the mind works. What renders a thinker effective is the skill with which he selects at the outset those principles in relation to which his facts come subsequently to be arranged. Systematization—and of course our object all the time is that of systematizing our experience—implies inevitably the imposition from above of a classification of the material which that material can never by itself provide. The

* A word here to any philosopher who may be reading these very unphilosophical pages. I am limiting myself to the purely psychological aspect of the problem of knowledge. Our ideas regarding external reality may be of the order of 'constructs', or, again, it may be that, as the romantic philosophers taught, the whole of the manifest universe is an emanation from the ego. But the distinction still remains between a realistic and a phantastic conception of that which appears to consciousness. Even the Vedantist, who believes that all is *maya,* is careful to distinguish between dreams and waking experiences. Whatever the philosophical truth about a railway engine, it remains true that the man who confuses it with an elephant is maladjusted to reality.

perspicacious thinker is he who seems to know, by a kind of instinct, the directions in which the subject should be explored. He has what Mr Geoffrey Sainsbury has admirably characterized as 'an interrogative profundity'. He is led to pick out of the whole what Coleridge describes in *The Friend* as 'central phenomena', key positions, as it were, round which all the elements in the complex will group themselves in an orderly, readily comprehensible and significant pattern. His incisions are deftly made. He has an eye for the fundamental anatomy of the object. His units are strategically selected so that he is able to dispense in his calculations with all manner of irritating epicycles and parallaxes. He distinguishes at a glance the fundamental from the derivative.

On the other hand, the unskilled operator is always offering us a series of cross-sections which only serve to give us an illusory or a distorted view of the subject, impeding our intellectual transactions and leaving the more radical issues untouched. Such bungling may incidentally do a great deal of damage even upon the material plane. There seem, for instance, to be serious reasons for believing that during the Great War the medical profession in England, by obstinately adhering to the wrong classification of certain diseases, caused the death of thousands of innocent men.*

But what, we must now ask, is the condition of attaining to a direct rather than an illusory vision of reality? To this question all enlightened psychologists, ancient and modern, have returned a perfectly decisive answer: emancipation from the dominion exercised on the mind by the infantile, egoistical, phantastic self. Purify your nature and you will perceive things as they are. All human psychological attitudes can be ranged between two extremes. At one end there is that of the being who is so

* See Appendix to *The Meaning of Meaning,* by C. K. Ogden and I. A. Richards (1923).

completely cut off from reality that he views every object presented to him through the refracting medium of his private passions and desires. At the other we have the consciousness of God, to whom alone things appear as they really are in themselves. Our intellectual development may be considered as a painful passage from one of these poles in the direction of the other. And it is the consequence, essentially, of a progressive liberation from spiritual bondage. The mind does not 'grow'; it simply becomes more free to respond. This or that inhibition is removed, and then, as the phrase goes, 'the scales fall from our eyes' and we perceive what was always there before us had we only been aware of the fact. Is it not true that when a man attains to a more comprehensive understanding of some aspect or other of life, this is usually because the force of certain evidence has suddenly come to make a new appeal to his mind, because an accustomed object has presented a new facet to his attention? We stare uncomprehendingly at an arrangement of lines and figures, and it is only when some obstruction within us has been mysteriously removed that they spell out a portentous message to our souls.

It is being which conditions thought; not *vice versa.* What it is that impels an imaginative thinker to seize so infallibly upon the vital issues in the problem we do not know. But we are at least aware that he owes his perspicacity to a certain freedom deep within his being. Its quality is due to a virtue which existed within him before he sat down to think at all. Call it sincerity, integrity, or what you will; it does not matter. The essential point is that it is something by which the character of the man's thought is predetermined; his conscious mind can only evolve its combinations within the limits set to it by this profound, interior condition of being. In the end the man can only think what he *is.*

The conclusion which follows is that the fundamental

problem before every person who wishes to penetrate with his mind into reality is not intellectual but moral in character. The value of thought is determined by something which lies on a higher plane than thought itself. The real task before the thinker is not so much that of refining and polishing his mind as that of *becoming* something that possesses a spiritual significance. Then, and then only, will such mental powers as he is endowed with be employed with creative effect.

Are our modern intellectuals prepared to accept this conception of the relation existing between the mind and the soul? Not, it would appear, in any complete sense. They are alive, of course, to the negative principle that our reasoning can be perverted by our desires. But they shrink from taking the further step of recognizing that if the mind can be prostituted to the service of the passions, its powers can equally be enhanced as the result of a more complete integration of the self. They fail to face the fact that, just as a man owes whatever degree of intellectual freedom he already possesses to a certain emancipation from his infantile self, so also it is to a still further degree of emancipation from that self that he must look if he wishes to penetrate more deeply into reality. They recognize clearly enough that if ever he falls below a certain standard of intellectual integrity it is for psychological reasons, but they wrongfully assume that any progress he may make in a forward direction is to be secured, not by a further purification of his being, but by the perfection of his mental processes.

2. The Unified Consciousness

We accept, then, the principle that the act of understanding is one in which the whole man is involved. Illumination is conditional upon inward purification; until the spirit is stirred the mind will remain undiscerning. It is in the nature of things that no specifically human problem will yield up its secrets to us unless our hearts are involved in the process of dealing with it. The object of our study is a being in whom instinct has flowered into consciousness, and it is a necessary conclusion that only by drawing upon both our passional and our intellectual natures can we hope to comprehend his character. Only to a binocular vision will the significance of man be revealed; we must observe him simultaneously through the lens of the discriminating mind and that of the sympathetic heart.

Every failure of the mind to deal effectively with its experience can be traced to a lack of balance between two great potencies in the soul, one masculine and positive, the other feminine and negative, in character. There is, in the first place, that within us which is responsive to whatever belongs to order, which seeks always to create unity within diversity, which looks everywhere for basic principles, which finds its satisfaction in establishing hierarchies and rearing architectonic structures. And there is that in us also which is poignantly alive to the precious character of the momentary and the individual, which has no disposition to dissociate the universal from the particular in which it appears, which is as vividly aware of the uniqueness of each several tree as it is indifferent to the wood of which it is a part.

When either of these sides of the intellectual nature acquires an undue ascendency over the other the result is a distorted view of reality. If the 'masculine' note is overstressed, we are met with academic or doctrinaire thinking, with logicality at the expense of faithfulness to experience, with an excessive tendency towards schematization and mechanization, with the sacrifice of flexibility, richness, and warmth to correctness and formal consistency—in a word, with an abuse of the powers of the reason. If, on the other hand, it is the 'feminine' element which is excessively stressed, we have an undue immersion in the immediate, an overpowering of the mind by the senses and its servitude to the phenomenal, the multiple, and the concrete. The result is sensationalism in literature, empiricism in science, and subjectivism in philosophy.

To achieve any understanding of life which is at all penetrating it is necessary that these two tendencies should be in a perfect state of equilibrium. The individual must somehow have effected a synthesis between the positive and the negative elements in his being. Then only will he be neither blinded by the transcendental perfection of the Word nor seduced by the insistent immediacies of the Flesh. While his vision of universal principles will be constantly enriched through the passion with which he concentrates upon the individual manifestation, his power to elucidate the significance of the isolated event will be enhanced through the fact that he is constantly alive to the superior reality of the Whole. In fine, to become aware of the deeper meaning of existence it is necessary to attain to that polarization of the heart and the head which only the mature artist and the enlightened mystic can be said to achieve with any degree of completeness. Out of this consciousness there comes, not only all true art and religion, but also all true science and philosophy. The head must work in and through the heart, the heart in and through the head. The truth about life is as completely hidden from woman with her native understanding of substance as it is from man with his native understanding of form. Only to that dualistic male-female being which is born of the regeneration of the soul can it be revealed in all its fulness.

Now it is pretty plain that so far as the present generation is concerned the disturbance which has taken place in the equilibrium between the heart and the head is definitely in one direction—towards an excessive degree of cerebration. As Mr Fausset has written in his *Proving of Psyche*, 'the soul of the modern man is at strife primarily with his mind and only secondarily with the flesh as the mind analyzes, exploits, or perverts its impulses'. Directly a person receives the smallest amount of education today the danger is that his consciousness will become inordinately mental, that he will regulate his behaviour from this one centre alone instead of that other centre which becomes active with the unification of the being. He will become idea-ridden, he will act on principles rather than on inspiration, he will become cut off from the deeper sources of his vitality and deteriorate into that unhappy product of modernity whose condition moved D. H. Lawrence to such despair.

Hence it is that the first task which today confronts those who are defending the claims of this unified consciousness is that of indicating as clearly as possible the limitations of this excessively cerebral attitude to experience. In another age, perhaps, the most urgent need might be to induce people to give their neglected heads a chance. But in these days of arid intellectualism it is clear that the emphasis must be differently placed. We have behind us several centuries of one-sided concentration upon the concrete, external aspects of existence, and it is imperative that the balance should be redressed.

3. Science and Inspiration

What has been the result of this in application, and first of all in the social sciences? As I have already dealt with this subject at considerable length in my *Learned Knife*, I will only treat it here in the briefest possible fashion.

It is impossible to study the development of such modern sciences as anthropology, economics, and psychology without receiving a powerful impression that the palpable confusion which prevails in them is traceable to limitations in the psychology of the anthropologists, economists, and psychologists themselves. With the steadily increasing secularization of our thought since the beginning of the modern scientific age we have come to accept more and more completely the assumption that the qualifications for elucidating truth in every sphere of enquiry are almost purely intellectual. And that assumption is becoming every year demonstrably more false. We are finding that the patient multiplication of observations can bring no really fruitful results unless it is conjoined with spiritual vision. And it is spiritual vision which the workers in this field most conspicuously lack. Fundamentally unilluminated, they fail, in spite of all their industry, to light upon the really vital categories, to pick out of the fabric those patterns which are most significant for our human purposes.

The fact is being forced upon us that what we are in need of today, even in the purely scientific field of sociology, is people who by some means or other have become quickened, people who have found themselves on a deeper level, people whose perceptions have been sharpened and whose minds have been fertilized because they have undergone a process of regeneration. One perceives here the significance of such a man as the late Walther Rathenau. As his biographer points out,* his whole conception of the social problem was based upon his acceptance of certain principles which he regarded as being operative in the communal and the personal life alike, and which he first apprehended in passing through the throes of a spiritual crisis in his thirty-ninth year. It is this *type* of experience which is so very badly needed by the world today. The real problem before us is not that of extending the range of our explorations upon the

* *Walther Rathenau,* by Count Harry Kessler (1929), p. 92.

plane on which they are at present being pursued, but that of encouraging the genesis of a kind of thinking which has its origin in an elevation of consciousness. Otherwise we shall end by being swamped in a vast mass of facts which reveal nothing because they have been amassed by minds which have no deep sense of reality to guide them in their enquiries.

Significant in this connexion is the increasing distrust which people are beginning to feel today for the findings of the 'expert'. Our specialists are continually assuring us that the issues at stake are almost incredibly complicated; there are only a few men in England, for instance, who are really able to understand the workings of the banking system. The science of economics is unbelievably intricate. And it is the same thing with the cure of disease, the education of the young, and almost everything else. The only people who have any legitimate claim to deal with these matters are those who have familiarized themselves with a vast technical literature, who conduct their discussions in an unintelligible jargon, whose mental processes are all but incomprehensible to the man in the street.

Yet may it not be after all that these experts of ours are to a large degree creating the complications which they find so bewildering? At the bottom of our minds most of us have an obstinate conviction that the fundamental issues are really perfectly simple, and that once they are glimpsed all these formidable intricacies will disappear. We feel that our specialists have lost themselves in a maze of contradictions and inconsistencies for the plain reason that they lack that purity of being which brings with it the power of seeing things simply. It is because the head is working divorced from the heart that the difficulties which it encounters are so prodigious. We have a strong impression that if the experts would cultivate something more fundamental than intellectual dexterity they would discover that the whole character of their problems would be transformed.*

4. The Wisdom of the Heart

We assert, then, that even when the mind is engaged with the most material issues a deeper integration of the being cannot but result in a new order of vision. The man will think *differently*, even though he is dealing with problems of immigration or international finance. But it is, of course, in relation to the more interior aspects of life that the consequences of such integration will be most apparent. The immediate result is that the individual becomes more and more conscious of the inability of the secular, rationalistic intelligence to deal with fundamental realities, and at the same time more and more aware of the significance of those things which cannot be defined but only *shown*. And this means that he becomes increasingly sensitive to the importance of the language of art. For it is the function of art to convey by means of symbols the nature of those aspects of reality which cannot be described in terms of purely logical thought.

Not that in this sphere reason altogether fails us. But

* One cannot refrain from speculating, in this connexion, as to the future of such a group as that which expresses its attitude in an obscure, but singularly interesting and alert, little quarterly, *Purpose*. The ideas advanced by these young men on such subjects as sociology and psychology strike one as being as intelligent as they are revolutionary. It is further manifest that they have all developed a definitely spiritual type of consciousness. And this gives their activity very great significance. It is thinkers of this stamp who are most probably destined to exert the dominant intellectual influence in the period on which we are entering. The merely clever people have by now discredited themselves so thoroughly as to convince even their own kind that something more fundamental is required if our problems are to be solved.

even the small measure of success which it achieves is secured only at the cost of a marked modification of its habitual processes. Being is dynamic, thought static. Hence on the plane of science our most valuable conceptions are strictly logical. On the plane of the spiritual our most potent ideas are paradoxical—or at least can only be paradoxically expressed. 'Man is what he is potentially; he is that more truly than he is anything else'. So writes Mr Middleton Murry in a recent work, expressing at the same time a fear that the statement may appear meaningless to a certain type of mind. Inevitably it will. Yet the fact remains that as a piece of description on this level it is as exact, as satisfying, and as intelligible to every person whose consciousness is awakened to this aspect of reality as is the description by a scientist of the structure of a cell.

The truth is, we are involved with a different set of standards. What was gratifying precision in the field of physics becomes in this new sphere intolerable rigidity, while, on the other hand, such qualities as poetic suggestiveness and allusiveness, which are completely out of place in the laboratory, now become weapons of the greatest possible value. The very excellencies of the rationalist's style now begin to irritate instead of to charm us; that clear, hard, metallic way of thinking which gives us such satisfaction when we are concerned with atoms or nebulæ has now only the effect of misrepresenting the object with which we are dealing. We perceive that the principle of adaptation is no less valid in the world of thought than it is in that of physical life.

Consider only the vocabulary of spiritual discourse. It abounds with images drawn from the realm of organic life. Unfoldment, growth, germination, the waters of life, the breath of the spirit, the fires of purification, the inner sun, the night of the soul, the bread of Heaven—such terms, incomprehensible as they must necessarily appear to the uninitiated, are almost indispensable if we wish to communicate the nature of our deeper, inner experience. And even if we one day discard them it remains true that a new terminology can only be created by those who are acquainted with the processes to which they refer.

The point which I would particularly stress, however, is this. Mechanistic thinking about spiritual problems is not simply the result of an error of judgment, of an easily remediable misapprehension. The phenomenon can only be properly understood in terms of that integration of the consciousness which has already made such a large claim on our attention. Looking at the question from this standpoint, we cannot fail to perceive that such conceptions as those referred to above can only acquire significance for us when the operations of the intelligence have been quickened by an influx from the affective side of the nature. And that influx, again, can only take place when we are living on a relatively lofty plane, a plane on which the spirit is in a certain condition of tension. This tension, as every artist and mystic knows, is not only exhausting in itself, but is also not to be attained without a considerable measure of preliminary self-discipline; we are concerned with a phase of being in which the whole man is involved in the process of understanding. Mere patience and resourcefulness alone will not carry us to our goal.

When, on the contrary, the heart and the head have ceased to co-operate in this intensive manner the consequence is a descent to the plane of mechanism, to that plane on which the detached, rationalizing intelligence is naturally at home. And it is the plane also on which the material can be dealt with in an infinitely more easy fashion, for it is now the mind alone which is called upon to exert itself. But it leads inevitably to a loss of grip upon those vital elements in the problem to which the integrated consciousness alone is fully alive.

A more detailed discussion of the difficulties which are raised for us by the discontinuity between being and thought is unfortunately impossible in these pages. But I have, I hope, sufficiently indicated that the nearer we draw to the more central aspects of reality the more deeply does the 'heart' become involved in the process of apprehending truth. Our progress is towards the mystical and the ineffable.

And this fact has an important practical application. It is the central, interior elements in reality which determine the character of the remainder. What I have described as the 'unified consciousness' is concerned pre-eminently with the vital, regulative processes of life. With the help of the intellect alone man can deal effectively with the more mechanical aspects of experience. Admittedly even here the fact of spirituality must tell. But it certainly does not tell to the same degree as it does in connexion with those of a more significant order. The ignoble and the corrupt may be shut out from an understanding of the poetic and the mystical, but they are not precluded from dealing with problems of chemistry and physics. Yet at the same time the real key to the situation is always to be found in human relationships, and here the factor of the 'heart' demands to be taken into account. The use which men make of their minds is determined by the state of their emotions. The person whose aptitude lies in understanding and directing those emotions is the psychologist. And the psychologist who has not been spiritually quickened is no psychologist at all.

The manifold ways in which our control over the more fundamental issues in life is impeded by our failure to unify the consciousness need not be reviewed here. I will limit myself to adducing two cases in point: that of the 'high-brow', and that of the philosophical thinker.

5. The Psychology of the High-brow

Whenever an individual displays to an inordinate degree a tendency to treat his experience in cerebral terms we meet with the phenomenon of the 'high-brow'. The 'high-brow' is the person who for some reason or other has permitted that part of his mind which exercises itself in analysis and classification to become unco-ordinated with those more delicate organs which serve to bring him into sympathetic rapport with his environment. His mind may be both subtle and powerful, but because its operations are insufficiently conditioned by emotion they fail to produce any really satisfying fruits.

Both the tendency towards undue intellectualism and that towards the thoroughpaced naturalism which is its complement have been abundantly exemplified in the course of our cultural history. Yet it remains true that the designation of 'high-brow', so far from being simply a new name for a familiar phenomenon, must be regarded rather as a term which has been coined in order to deal with a type that is substantially *new*. And the newness lies in the fact that we are today confronted with a marked tendency among our more serious and intellectual men and women towards a kind of spiritual anæmia. The more intelligent they are and the more seriously they show themselves to be concerned with the deeper problems of modern life, the more do their thinking and writing betray a nerveless, cold, morbidly scrupulous and sterile quality. Hence the suspicion with which their productions are regarded by the masses, who have always had an infallible flair for any deficiency in vitality, in whatever form it may appear.

Not that the true facts of the case are immediately apparent to the uninitiated. The ordinary intelligent but not highly sophisticated person when he is presented with any intellectual performance which seems to have about it an unduly frigid and forbidding character is charitable enough to assume that his misgivings may be unjustified. If I was more clever, he says to himself, I should be able to see that all this refined analysis, this disdainful repudiation of inferior standards, this pressing home of subtle distinctions, is really as important as it is made out to be. Yet all the time a still, small voice is whispering in his ear that his instincts are telling him the truth: these people are sick souls. If they had really gained a vision of deeper truths which have escaped the majority, their presentation of them ought somehow, he feels, to come out *differently*. Why, when they try to share with him their secrets, does he, Mr Everyman, feel so bewildered and ill at ease—and remain in the end with his hunger unsatisfied? The cause of his distress may, perhaps, become more clear if, making use of the high-brow's favourite weapon, we undertake a brief analysis of the intellectualist's attitude to the world.

The function of the discursive intelligence is that of a servant. We are obliged to dissect our experience in order to discover what it entails for us. From this point of view the more detached and clear-headed we can be the better. But this is not to say that intellectualism is a substitute for vision. It is desirable to give one's self a clear account of what one has seen. But no ability in this respect will compensate for the fact that one's vision is naturally poor. And this is where the weakness of the average intellectual lies. He is incredibly precise, but precise regarding data of a relatively insignificant order. It is, indeed, just because his data are so insignificant that he expends such inordinate efforts in subjecting them to analysis.

As conceived of by the really thoroughbred member of the intelligentsia, the business of conveying our thoughts and feelings to others is one of quite remarkable difficulty. Our communication with one another is extremely imperfect, for the reason that the language of nearly all of us is, without our knowing it, either 'emotive' or at least dreadfully ambiguous, appropriate perhaps to the informal purposes of conversation, but lacking in that degree of precision which is called for in science and philosophy.

Up to a point the charge is not without justice. Certainly for every attempt to clarify thought we should be deeply grateful. But at the same time it remains true that the normal mode of understanding for human beings is that of *sight*. The more our spiritual life unfolds, the more do things reveal their character to us directly without there being any occasion for recourse to extrinsic evidence; as our vision deepens we find that it approximates more and more closely to that angelic intuition for which demonstration and analysis are unnecessary. Now intuition is closely associated with sympathy, so that we find that to the degree that sympathy fails we are constrained to fall back upon analysis and explanation. In terms of personal relationships this principle finds expression in the fact that the need which we experience to define our terms is the measure of our alienation from our fellow-men. We are compelled to have recourse to precision because we are spiritually remote from the person whom we are addressing, because one or both of us have failed in 'empathy'. Our need to formulate our ideas with exactness is the offspring of our separation, just as the number of clauses in a contract is proportionate to the mutual distrust between its signatories. If we are listening to a person with insight and sympathy we are able to read his individual symbols, to estimate the peculiar significance which he attaches to standardized terms, to penetrate behind his language into his being. For lovers speech may become unnecessary, or even a positive impediment to expression.

It will thus become apparent why the typical intellectual sets such store upon scientific and philosophical precision in language: it is a measure which is immediately called for whenever there is a need to convey the character of a situation to an unperceptive mind. For one finds that it is the unsympathetic, the self-centred, and the unimaginative who are always demanding definition and precision and finding every other statement either equivocal or obscure. Such people are driven to being terribly intelligent just because they are naturally so terribly obtuse. Being incapable of *sight*—which, as I say, is the natural mode of apprehending the nature of what is before one—they are impelled to call more and more clamorously for vexatious explanations as to what has been 'meant'. It is as if every time there was a question of asking one's neighbour to pass the salt at dinner one was obliged to safeguard oneself from misinterpretation by recalling its chemical formula. A conversation with a real intellectual gives rise to a situation of very much the same order. For the plain fact is that he is deficient in imaginative sympathy. He has no comprehension of anything but the purely verbal content of any statements which are made to him. A whole series of alternative interpretations open themselves fan-wise before his mind, each of which appears to him as being equally plausible, so that nothing remains for him but to discover, by laborious cross-questioning, what it was that the speaker intended to convey. No one of them has any more probability for him than any other; no one of them is seen to be excluded in the light of evidence which would be there for a more sensitive spirit. As a result he tends to fall very readily into the error of concluding that the understanding of others is an affair of dexterity, subtlety, and logicality, instead of being primarily a matter of sympathy and love.*

* The point is aptly illustrated in the course of a recent notice in *The Times Literary Supplement* of Mr William

The real reason for the intellectual's failure to deal with his experience is apparent enough: he is more interested in ideas than in people. Hence, instead of treating every expression of thought and feeling by others as first of all a means towards perfecting what is really a mystical form of communion with another human soul, he treats them first of all in so far as they can be said to have an existence in themselves, wilfully detached from the consciousness from which they originally emanated. For him all utterances have become *anonymous*. His point of departure is no longer the thinker but the thought, which he does not consider in relation to the mind which gave it birth, but from the point of view of the place which it is seen to occupy in some abstract scheme. He is, in fact, only interested in ideas when they are already *dead,* when, like fish that are dying on dry land, they have lost all those radiant hues with which they were enriched when they were in their natural element. Then, when they have been translated to the plane of the abstract, he proceeds to relate them, ingeniously and elaborately, to all manner of others, thereby bringing into existence a whole series of problems, com-

Empson's *Seven Types of Ambiguity.* Commenting upon a passage in which the author draws attention to certain obscurities in a poem by George Herbert, the reviewer observes: 'For, after all, a poem is a poem not least by virtue of its power to ward off these vagaries of the intellect. It is to some degree an incantation, a word of immediate power, compelling the wandering mind to response of a certain order; and only so far as the receiving mind restrains its speculations within the limits of this order is it speculating about the poem at all'. The issue could not be more happily defined. And the principle which is valid for the realm of poetry is equally valid for the realm of life: the effect of imaginative sympathy is to inhibit, and at the same time to direct into a creative channel, the activity of the speculative intellect.

plications, and perspectives which come to have more significance for him than the realities which provided the basis for their creation.*

It is in the nature of the case that the character of the disease with which our modern intellectuals are afflicted should have been analyzed with remarkable skill by the patients themselves. For one thing, they are in a position to watch the process of their spiritual disintegration from within. For another, they are far too intelligent not to perceive where the root of their troubles lies. Nevertheless, it is extremely interesting to find that their conclusions are being confirmed independently by others working in a completely different field.

I allude to the testimony of the therapeutist. And I will illustrate my meaning by reference to an article which recently appeared in the *British Journal of Medical Psychology* (Vol. IX, Part II, 1929) from the pen of a young London specialist, Dr E. Graham Howe. It bears the somewhat forbidding title of 'Compulsive Thinking as a Castration Equivalent', but its significance for our present enquiry is considerable.

Dr Howe, although obviously an exceptionally intelligent man, is just as obviously the last person to whom one would apply the designation of 'high-brow' in any depreciatory sense. His interest in the afflictions of the

* The attitude is very accurately conveyed in the following passage from Mr Aldous Huxley's *Point Counterpoint* (1928): 'All that the intelligence could seize upon he seized. She reported to him her intercourse with the natives of the realm of emotion and he understood at once, he generalized her experience for her, he related it with other experiences, classified it, found analogies and parallels. From single and individual it became in his hands part of a system. She was astonished to find that she and her friends had been, all unconsciously, substantiating a theory, or exemplifying some interesting generalization'.

intelligentsia was only aroused in a perfectly natural manner in the course of his professional practice. Amongst his patients were a number of people who were at once singularly unhappy and abnormally active intellectually, though in a palpably sterile manner. A study of their symptoms served to turn his attention to the wider problems presented by the psychology of the type:

> What is the psycho-pathology of the 'high-brow'? That is the simplest form the question takes. Is there a quest for thinking for the sake, not of the thought, but of the escape that thinking brings? . . . Is the whole process of thought itself compulsive in some cases? If so, what is the unconscious motive, and what the end that compulsive thinking seeks to gain?

His conclusions, as the following passages show, are of remarkable interest:

> The motive of compulsive thinking is, on this hypothesis, escape from guilt by a mechanism of castration, the equivalent of which is by de-emotionalization and intellectualization, the one leading inevitably to the other. . . . The primary motive is escape from guilt, which is obtained by the substitution of a more civilized and socially tolerated process of thought for the infantile and guilty process of feeling.

And again:

> Compulsive thinking is more than a problem in individual psycho-pathology, for its principle permeates the foundations of society and threatens it with suicide, through the underlying castration motive. Compulsive thinkers tend to become the teachers of the race. The result is the dogmatic commendation of over-intellectualization, emotional maladjustment, mechanization, and a confusion of precept that threatens the root of the true principles of education, religion, and sound pyschological development, which must be *emotional* freedom and growth.
>
> In a scientific method, reason and mathematical accuracy are not enough, for the motive of each may be *unconscious*

and compulsive, seeking an escape from the problem which they seem to try to solve. The beginning and the end of life is a problem of *emotional* development, and faith and love must be the beginning and the end of our search for truth.

It is quite possible that after all life and love and growth may be simple things, capable of comprehension by cottage wisdom and faith; but we are *taught* confusion through the mechanizations of compulsive thought.

One hesitates, naturally, to base any extensive conclusions upon a solitary article in a psychological journal. But it does seem to be one of those significant little indications which show which way the wind is blowing.

6. Philosophy and Human Experience

The consequences of a failure to synthesize the intellectual with the affective nature are no less evident in the sphere of philosophy than in those of science or practical life.

Philosophy, as it is taught today in our universities, has about it a very definite character: it is conspicuously and monotonously 'pure'. I mean by this that our philosophers are concerned, not with attempting to introduce order into the totality of our experience as human beings, but with exploring the implications of a very small number of highly abstract concepts which can be identified by an elementary appeal to introspection. Indeed, there are certain of them, it appears, who are able to derive all the material they require for the purpose of their reflexions from being left alone in a room with a penny! The rest is a matter of logic, scrupulousness, and patience.

That the thinker of this type can do little to aid us in dealing with the actual problems with which life in the world presents us is obvious enough. And this, if he is intelligent, he will be perfectly prepared to admit. But he will probably also maintain that this fact does not affect in any serious fashion his ability to arrive at philosophical truth. For he takes his departure, knowingly or unknowingly, from a distinction between two outstanding modes of response to external reality, one emotional and the other intellectual, one that of the poet, the other that of the individual who has a 'speculative' mind. It is not the business of the poet to philosophize, while, on the other hand, the philosopher must be careful not to permit his thinking to be disturbed by the influence of passion. Their respective reactions to life are, in fact, to be regarded as being essentially complementary.

It is important to take note of what this theory implies. It implies that a person is sufficiently qualified for thinking philosophically about the Universe provided only that he possesses a certain purely intellectual endowment. His principal weapons are logic, analytical power, the capacity to manipulate abstract concepts. The fact that he may altogether lack the poetic consciousness is assumed not to *tell*—any more than it tells in the case of the mathematician. In other words, it is possible, on this view of the matter, to leave a whole side of one's nature undeveloped and yet to be able to attain to a true philosophical view of Reality. Or, to put the matter somewhat differently, the province of philosophy is so conceived that the fact that an individual is possessed of such qualities as passion, poetic imagination, and moral depth does not confer any marked advantage upon him in dealing with it.

Whatever there is to be said for or against this notion on theoretical grounds, it cannot be denied that in practice it is widely acted upon. We accept almost without question the assumption that the qualifications required of the student of philosophy are of an extremely limited type. Just as we have come almost to take it for granted that there is something a little prim and mawkish about the style of the average minister of religion today, so also have we come to picture the 'philosopher' as a rather harmless, kindly, and desiccated person whose strength lies almost exclusively in his capacity to deal with abstruse theoretical problems which are beyond the comprehension of the lay mind. We do not find it incongruous that as a human being he may be pathetic and ineffective and lacking in insight into all but the most metaphysical problems.

But should not this state of affairs really make us feel somewhat uneasy? Does it not after all go to indicate that we have once more to do with the pernicious consequences of that secularizing of thought which has taken place in every field of enquiry since the Renaissance? Are we not tending to confuse the possession of a philosophical *technique* with the possession of philosophical *knowledge*?

Let us endeavour to keep the issues clear. Any confusion of the respective provinces of art and philosophy cannot but be fatal. The subject-matter of 'pure' philosophy must necessarily be a collection of highly abstract concepts—concepts which from one point of view can only be arrived at by transcending the plane of emotion. Yet at the same time it is also true that unless the experience which serves as the ultimate ground and basis for these abstract flights is both rich and comprehensive, the speculative ideas which result will inevitably be insufficiently vital and central. The only philosophizing that is worth having is that which has come into being through the individual's expressing in terms of severely abstract thought a consciousness which might alternatively, given another type of temperament, have expressed itself in terms of poetic creation. Or, to put it quite simply, however much a philosophical system may *appear* to be the product of 'pure speculation', its significance is dependent as much upon its creator's emotional as upon his intellectual endowment. The only philosophy that counts is the philosophy which, however transcendental the issues with which it deals, yet symbolizes the individual's reaction to the impact of a complete human experience.

As to the character which is conferred upon a man's speculative thinking by the fact that his heart has been awakened as well as his head, this is a question on which I do not feel properly qualified to speak. But I would venture to suggest that the fact that his consciousness has become enriched cannot but find a reflexion in the character of the elements which he regards as being constitutive of reality. The more deeply he penetrates into the depths of his own being, the more profoundly will his conception of the world outside himself become modified. If a person has no deep sense of the mystery of personality, of the operation within himself of the factors of will and emotion, he will naturally tend to present us with a Universe in the shaping of which these elements have not played an important part. An impoverished self will be led inevitably to postulate an impoverished not-self as its complement.

Again, it would seem that a philosopher who is emotionally profound should be difficult to understand—difficult, that is to say, in the sense that the ordinary type of philosophical thought is *not* difficult to understand. And it should be difficult—for the unawakened—for exactly the same reason that the utterances of the poet and the mystic are difficult: because, representing as it does the fruits of the responsiveness of the heart as well as the operations of the mind, it can only be assimilated at the cost of something more exhausting than purely intellectual labour. I speak with great diffidence, but I must say that it appears to me that a great deal of the so-called obscurity in Coleridge's metaphysics can be traced to the fact that his thinking on these matters, although strictly philosophical, is the result of an attempt to give intellectual form to the products of a consciousness which was infinitely more full and rich than that of the ordinary philosopher. Hence the difficulty in following his thought which is experienced by those people for whom the study of philosophy is an activity that can be pursued irrespective of one's development in other directions.

This also is plain. To be a poet is to have a heightened awareness of unity. And this, again, is to become concerned with conceptions which cannot be effectively expressed in terms of analytical thought. It is, indeed, just the office of the poet to bring to life for us those aspects of existence with which the imagination alone can deal. It follows inescapably, therefore, that any philosophy which has its roots in the poetic consciousness must exhibit an anti-rationalistic tendency. That is to say, it will utilize all the resources of reason to substantiate the fact that the nature of Reality cannot be fully apprehended by the exercise of the reason alone. It will be constrained to recognize the existence of an intuitive faculty which transcends that by the exercise of which its own conclusions are arrived at. Its demonstrations will culminate, like those of Plato, in the recognition of the validity of certain principles whose operation can only be conveyed by resorting to allegory and myth. It will flower finally into the poetry in which, for all its strictly logical character, it will all the time have had its roots.

Finally, to whatever degree the true philosopher may occupy himself with problems of a purely intellectual nature, the spiritual inspiration of his thinking will always, one feels, be indicated by the fact that he possesses the capacity to bring his metaphysics into a fruitful relationship with the most humble and ephemeral circumstances of life. His affinities will be with such thinkers as Pascal, Nietzsche, Schopenhauer, and Coleridge. For, as we have conceived him, his mind will have been stirred into its most profound activity owing to his having looked at the world through the eyes of a poet—and the mark of the poet is that he apprehends the universal imaginatively by studying those natural forms in which the character of the Infinite is reflected. It is just because in his thinking he has taken his departure from life in all its richness that he is able to bring his conclusions so widely to bear upon it. The range of the phenomena which he is able to interpret as the result of his speculations is determined by the range of the phenomena of which he initially took account in embarking upon them. His wisdom is like the rain, which fertilizes the earth from which its moisture was originally derived.

CHAPTER III

LEARNING AND LEADERSHIP

IN the last chapter I advanced the view that, since thought must be regarded as a function of being, the determining factor in our understanding of life is ultimately moral. It is clear that if once we accept this principle we shall be obliged to look at the problem of intellectual leadership in an entirely new light. For we shall find ourselves demanding of the man who concerns himself with social and cultural problems that he lay a foundation for his work by submitting himself to a definite type of spiritual discipline, since it is on such discipline that insight in the end depends.

My aim in what follows is to give this question a practical application by enquiring how far the obvious failure of our modern intellectuals to help us in dealing with our experience may not be due to their reluctance to adopt this wider view of their responsibilities. In other words, my theme is that which has already been developed so brilliantly by M. Julien Benda in his *Trahison des Clercs*.* But this able critic limited his attention almost exclusively to the *clercs* of his own country, whose shortcomings strike one as being peculiarly Gallic in character. His indictment, therefore, although it raises many issues which may well make our intellectuals pause and reflect, is not really relevant to the Anglo-Saxon situation. Hence I make no apology for considering the problem anew.

1. THE PROBLEM OF VALUES

That the function of the modern critic is definitely changing in character is evident enough. The obliga-

* Translated under the title of *The Great Betrayal* (1928).

tions which are laid upon him in the present age are at once more exacting and more extensive than those which his predecessors of an earlier epoch were called upon to meet. The critic, for instance, who is content today to confine his attention to the purely æsthetic aspects of literature already belongs, in a sense, to an era that is past. Such writers as the late Sir Edmund Gosse, for whom the world of letters was a region which existed by itself dissociated from all other aspects of existence, secured their prestige on what we should today be inclined to regard as unduly easy terms.

For we live in an age of Science. It has become an almost instinctive impulse with us to deal with every problem presented to us in relation to the conclusions which have been reached by investigators in the most diverse branches of research. Although we are today interested in personalities to an exceptional degree, we are not satisfied until we have considered them not only in and for themselves, but in respect, also, to the place which they occupy in the sociological, the biological, or the psychological scheme. We wish to interpret the phenomenon in terms of wider processes of life, to pass beyond it into more general considerations, to gain from it light on more comprehensive issues.

This urge to unify our experience, to look everywhere for the working of deeper laws of life beneath the picturesque surface which we were previously content to contemplate in purely æsthetic terms, is, one feels, expressive of a real growth of consciousness. But it means also that the critic must be prepared to study in fields far removed from that of pure literature, that he must possess a really extensive erudition. Otherwise his pronouncements will fail to arrest our attention.

Yet even when our intellectual enjoys sufficient leisure to render himself comparatively well-informed, his task has only begun. It is not enough for him to be properly orientated, to deal with his subject in the light of the findings of the philosophers, the economists, and the theologians. He must provide us with values as well. He must give us light on what is to be regarded as ultimately satisfying and desirable in life.

And here he usually disappoints us. For we find that the tendency of all but a small minority of our modern critics is to accept their values ready-made from the historians, the anthropologists, the psychologists, and the industrialists by whom they have been given currency. They are standing on exactly the same level as those people whose productions they are endeavouring to evaluate, permitting themselves to be dictated to in just that one province in which they should normally speak with authority. Although in the course of their criticism they are expert enough in placing the object against the background of modern thought, it does not occur to them to submit that background itself to serious examination. They possess no points of reference beyond the sphere of the immediate and the contemporary in respect to which they can orientate themselves. They are overpowered by actuality and can, therefore, throw no light upon the deeper nature of our experience.

This is a serious situation. It is absolutely impossible for us to get along without the aid of certain people who can be trusted to speak with authority on the vitally important question of human ends. The scientist provides us with extensive enough information regarding what *is,* but unless we have those among us who tell us also what makes for, and what does not make for, our more fundamental well-being, we are lost.

In the Middle Ages all questions of value were decided by the Church, which was the recognized custodian of the whole life of man, material, social, and spiritual; nowadays the Pope, in making enactments regarding the seemly length for a woman's skirt, is only endeavouring to maintain the same tradition in a world that has decided, for better or worse, to look after such matters for itself. But today, in an age in which ecclesiastical authority has lost all its prestige, the function of the Church has been taken over by the secular thinker. It is to him that we now turn for instruction on the subject of values, and if he fails us there is nobody else to whom we can confidently look for aid. The initiative has passed from the priests to the critics, philosophers, and artists, who now occupy an extremely important position in the order, or disorder, of modern society.

The view that I am advancing is that our modern intellectuals have never really brought themselves to face the nature of the responsibility that has thus fallen upon their shoulders. And, as a result, they are continually disappointing us, not in respect of their purely intellectual competence, which is adequate enough, but in respect of sheer spiritual endowment. In every case in which they fail us the cause of their defection is to be found in lack of moral depth.

2. The Architecture of Humanism

Take first the problem of architectonics. One cannot study the writings of our modern humanistic critics with any attention without being struck by the singular fact that the majority of them fail notably to attain to a truly 'humanistic' attitude to the world. This is all the more surprising because it is, after all, the peculiar function of this type of thinker to achieve centrality, to preserve his sense of proportion to an outstanding degree, to do justice to all the diverse needs and potencies of the spirit. It is he more than anyone who ought to be capable of putting things in their right place.

Not, of course, that our modern intellectuals disappoint us here in any very obvious way. Their standards are, as a whole, those of highly cultivated men. If we enquire of them concerning the respective parts which should be played in an enlightened society by, say, such elements as Protestant fervour, detective fiction, sexual gratification, and Mr Bernard Shaw, the best of them can be depended upon to give us answers that indicate that they are in possession of reputable standards. In relation to the outlook of the great mass of humanity today, their standpoint—and we are duly grateful for the fact—is that of a really discriminating minority.

Where they fail us is in respect of more delicate issues. For although they have succeeded in avoiding all the more obvious types of fanatical allegiance, they do, nevertheless, yield to the temptation of exaggerating the significance of some limited principle, rational, moral, or æsthetic, in relation to the problem of regenerating society. In scriptural terms, they are guilty in one form or another of idolatry. They demand from culture a more profound inspiration than it is legitimate to expect; or they put forward as a complete humanism what is really a dangerous exaltation of the rational side of the nature; or they depend to an excessive degree upon the findings of intuition. In a word, they fall away, in one direction or another, from their own humanistic standards.

That there is a virtue in prejudice I am among the first to admit. Indeed, on another page I have advanced the view that it is of an increased amount of prejudice that our more sophisticated men and women are most urgently in need today. But while the affirmation of an individualistic attitude is appropriate enough in its place, it acquires a very different significance in the case of critics who have taken upon themselves the responsibility of influencing the intellectual life of their age. Their first obligation is that of being scrupulously fair in their judgments. And, from this point of view, I think that the achievements of our modern intellectuals are very far from satisfying. On every hand one is offered some one-sided, egoistically determined, and usually plausibly enunciated philosophy, the character of which is in the last resort the expression of individual bias. We have Mr Bertrand Russell urging upon us that we should devote ourselves to securing ends which can only appeal to the purely rationalistic mind. We have Mr J. C. Powys seductively displaying the impossibly Pagan faith of the sensationalist. We have Mr Clive Bell commending to us another form of sensationalism of a less attractive order. We have Mr Joseph Wood Krutch confessing to a hopeless pessimism which seems to have its origin in a misinterpretation of the import of the findings of science. We have Mr Wyndham Lewis wasting his brilliant talents in misdirected satire. We have Mr Babbitt preaching to us an intolerably narrow ethical philosophy. We have Mr Middleton Murry advancing an almost fanatically extreme view of the significance of the poetical experience.

All of these people are sincere, and all of them have valuable things to tell us. But, without exception, they leave us uneasy and unappeased in the end, and this for the reason that no one of them has attained to any real centrality of vision. They are none of them capable of that true justice which comes from first penetrating deeply into a wide range of divergent attitudes and then achieving a true synthesis between them. They are most of them simply pronouncing individual manifestoes. On the other hand, the only writers today who do contrive to be wide in their sympathies are able to achieve nothing much more than the superficial tolerance of the academic thinker who sees only the external aspects of the objects which he is comparing. And this is not justice, but liberalism at its worst.

Now all this, it may well seem, simply amounts to saying that true culture is exceedingly difficult to achieve.

But there is more involved. Once again we find ourselves coming back to the religious experience. For it can hardly escape our attention that the problem of preserving humanistic standards uncorrupted presents more difficulties in an age which has become indifferent to the appeal of religion than it does in a period in which religious principles form the accepted basis of culture. And the reason is plain. In a religious epoch the most urgent demand of the spirit—that of having a supreme end to which it can dedicate all its manifold activities—receives complete satisfaction, and, as a result, there is comparatively little danger of the significance of any one mode of human expression being either inordinately exaggerated on the one hand or unduly neglected on the other. The uncultivated will always, as one is aware, go to painful extremes; it is their way. But it is hardly too much to say that, given an approximately equal degree of education, the man who is religious will, just through the fact that everything in the world has become for him related to one Centre, find less difficulty in preserving a truly humanistic attitude to experience.

Certainly it is a notable fact that established religion and a high type of humanistic culture tend to be found in association. The educated Catholic, for instance, is basing his life on a philosophy which simply compels him to do justice to the different sides of our nature. The interest which is being shown today in the Scholastic Philosophy constitutes, one feels, a real tribute to the superior insight of Religion; the secular mind finds itself obliged to recognize that the man whose eyes are steadily directed to an Absolute which lies above the plane of ordinary experience, proves capable, paradoxically enough, of evaluating that experience in singularly accurate terms. Conversely, it is typical of an age like the present, in which men possess no object of sovereign worth relative to which a hierarchy of values can be established, that it should abound in the most monstrous ideological growths.

There are, it is true, thinkers to be found among us who do contrive to maintain a truly humanistic attitude towards the world. The really balanced humanist is not altogether an extinct species. But he usually pays for his equilibrium by a corresponding deficiency in dynamic power. For the thinker who is actually capable of putting all the different varieties of human expression in their respective places is really evaluating them with reference to a central point of experience whose existence he implicitly affirms rather than immediately perceives. He is like a man who at dawn, while the sun itself is still hidden from his gaze, is yet able to observe the manner in which its rays are traversing the sky in different directions above the horizon. The particles of his experience have been polarized by a magnet whose existence has not been directly revealed to him, though its presence is implied by the type of order which he feels impelled to introduce into his experience. As to his emotions, his sympathies have been withdrawn from all one-sided modes of self-assertion, while he yet lacks that transcendental object by which they might be more deeply aroused. We can hardly regard him as a 'pure' humanist; it is only by virtue of his crypto-religiosity that he is enabled to be humanistic about Humanism itself.

3. Scepticism and Responsibility

There is a certain element of irony in the fact that the more 'advanced' our modern thinkers become, the more do they tend to emphasize the validity of certain principles first enunciated between two and three thousand years ago. The wheel has turned full circle: our twentieth-century experimentalism has brought us back to the point of recognizing that there is more in Confucius and

Aristotle than meets the positivistic eye. The path of scepticism is leading back to orthodoxy.

One cannot help observing, however, that the re-affirmation of these venerable truths by our critics has little dynamic force. For they are pleading for certain principles, not so much because they have found within themselves a new source of truth and power, as because they have been driven willy-nilly to the conclusion that nothing but the acceptance of such doctrines would seem to fit the case. There is little spring or radiance in their apologetics; they are simply presenting us with what remains on their hands when all the other alternatives have been exhausted. Their eyes are drawn to no bright and inspiring object which attracts them on the horizon of the future; they are not pouring new wine into the old bottles; their pronouncements are rather the expression of discouragement and fatigue. Nothing, it appears, will save the situation but a return to the values of 'high religion'—the tone is very much that of a committee who have satisfied themselves that all but one system of concrete paving have disappointed our expectations. And the effect of their verdict upon us is correspondingly feeble.

If, however, we venture to complain of the negativity of his attitude, the modern intellectual usually replies that the matter is out of his control. The only standpoint possible for the really sophisticated thinker today is one of profound scepticism. The issues are far too complicated to justify one in holding any positive beliefs. The position, in fact, is that once defined with admirable clearness by Mr T. S. Eliot in No. 1 of Mr Wyndham Lewis's *The Enemy*:

> It takes application, and a kind of genius, to believe anything, and to believe *anything* (I do *not* mean merely to believe in some 'religion') will probably become more and more difficult as time goes on. . . . We await, in fact . . .

the great genius who shall triumphantly succeed in believing *something*. For those of us who are higher than the mob, and lower than the man of inspiration, there is always doubt; and in doubt we are living parasitically (which is better than not living at all) on the minds of the men of genius of the past who have believed something.

Now, from one point of view, this scepticism is commendable enough. It indicates the fact that the 'acids of modernity' have done their work thoroughly. The man's attitude may be desolatingly negative (it is, of course, no longer the attitude of Mr Eliot himself), but the ground is at least cleared for the creation of something new. His very extremity may presage an impending revelation.

Here, however, we are obliged to take account of the element of morality. To reject, conscientiously and comprehensively, is a salutary procedure. But a man cannot afford to wander endlessly in the desert of relativities in which he finds himself as a result. Something must be *done*. It is not enough to complain that the intellect is impotent before the mass of contradictions which are presented to us by our modern experience. The intellect is only a part of the man; there are other organs at his disposal for apprehending the nature of reality. There lies before him the task of achieving a new synthesis. In other words, he must tread courageously the perilous road which has already been followed by such uncompromising modernists as Mr Murry and Mr Fausset.

My complaint against the average modern intellectual is that he is content to remain, not without a certain complaisance, in the no-man's land of disillusion. If, he argues, I can *see* nothing ahead of me, what else is there for me to do? The answer can only be that the admission reveals the superficiality of his scepticism. To doubt sincerely and consistently is to be in Hell. And this is insupportable. If the suspension of belief is honest, the outcome must either be a paralyzing despair or a birth into a new mode of consciousness.

And this brings us back to the moral responsibility of the modern intellectual. As the experience of generations of finely tempered spirits goes to show, the determining element in the discovery of truth is the *will*. There is also involved the important element of grace, but it is normally the activity of the will which prepares the way for its reception. However impotent the mind may find itself before Life, light will finally come if only the man dedicate the whole of his deeper being to the end of attaining to truth. Blindness is ultimately of the soul, vision the fruit, not merely of cerebration, but of sincere aspiration. If only the tension be sufficient, the inner demand for illumination persistently enough maintained, some type of liberation is bound to follow. The man will at last find himself able to make a positive affirmation.

I grant that the truth which he thus comes to possess may be narrow and one-sided. It probably will be. And this is from one point of view disappointing. For as I have already suggested, the obligation upon the critic is that of achieving centrality. But it remains true that even a partial vision is preferable to a sterile scepticism. The man who has won his way through to illumination is at least able to identify himself positively with some definite belief. And it is of such identification that we are desperately in need in these oppressively 'historical' times. We want, not estimates and calculations, but soul-knowledge. Even distorted and exaggerated beliefs are to be welcomed, if only they emanate from this deeper centre. For that which comes from the whole man, even if it be lacking in wisdom, will at least be vital and have the effect of calling out the deeper reality in others. In other words, there will be engendered a process of true dynamic opposition and mutual determination. Men will meet, differ, agree, on a really human level; not merely on the plane of the intellect. The transactions which take place will be between true individuals who have found themselves, instead of between disembodied intelligencies. And out of this association there may come the living truth of which we are in need.

4. Esoteric and Exoteric

But even when our modern intellectuals have attained to something of the nature of positive belief they are a long way from being able to exert any decisive influence upon the mass of mankind. What is more, their impotence in this respect seems to increase with the degree of their intelligence. The more subtle and penetrating the mind the more inaccessible are its ideas to the rest of the world. There is simply no effective mechanism available for putting them into general circulation. The writings of our most discerning thinkers are highly critical in character, demanding in the reader exceptional sensitiveness and subtlety; they abound in classical and philosophical references which can have little meaning for any but the *cognoscenti*; the problem is formulated and discussed in terms which are scarcely intelligible except to the most cultivated of readers.

Not, of course, that we can demand of our critics that they should write for the man in the street. Ideas, and particularly elusive and profound ideas, must necessarily be for the few. We neither expect, nor encourage, the office boy to ponder over the pages of M. Ramon Fernandez or Mr Eliot. Yet this circumstance does not prevent us from feeling that it is our critics themselves who are responsible for the fact that the influence which they exert is so restricted. We cannot resist the impression that they are making it all very much more difficult than it need be, and this for the reason that, owing to a certain limitation of their consciousness, they are only capable of conducting the discussion in excessively intellectualistic terms. Once again the heart has failed to co-operate with the head.

The truth is that the intellectualism of our critics represents to a large degree the rationalization of certain elementary movements in the soul, which in the case of the great majority of us do not need to be subjected to any such process. To put the matter in plain terms, all this fine analysis, all this talk about 'reason', 'values', and 'intelligence', is really nothing more than the form assumed among the *illuminati* by a simple urge towards goodness. It is an embellishment elaborated by the intelligentsia for its own satisfaction alone, an *édition de luxe* of the plain man's sympathy with decency and justice. The basic element in both is an inclination towards virtue. But whereas that inclination is revealed in the case of a more guileless soul by his straightforward approbation of right behaviour, it finds expression in that of the intellectual in such gestures as an endorsement of the judgments of Confucius, or an appreciation of the profundity of Aquinas.

Actually, intellectualism of this type is purely esoteric in its significance. But this is not to say that for a minority it does not perform a very important function. When an ordinary person becomes more humane in his outlook the change in his character takes place in a comparatively unobtrusive way. He becomes, quite simply, a more decent sort of person. In the case of the intellectual, on the contrary, it cannot accomplish itself without a complicated contrapuntal elaboration of the thematic material. The process does not seem real and convincing to him until he can envisage it in terms of the operation of principles which have been formulated in the past by 'the best minds'. Unless his findings are corroborated by theirs he has little confidence in them. He can only recognize the significance of his own feelings when they are reflected back to him from the mirror of antiquity. Then only does truth come for him to possess substance and dynamic power. That type of symbolization happens to be congenial to his understanding, where a homely instance or an eloquent allegory would be to another mind of a different stamp. He assimilates his Sunday School stories more readily when they are presented to him in terms of the Nichomachean Ethics or the Thomistic Synthesis. But the root of the matter is the same.

Our intellectuals are not so much penetrating to depths of understanding which are inaccessible to the less sophisticated; they are dealing with certain fundamentally simple issues in terms of a peculiarly complicated code. They are concerned, it is true, with certain delicate and truly important problems which only exist for the highly cultivated mind. But these refinements are not the main point. Not, at least, if we are looking at the question from the standpoint of regenerating our present civilization. For the substance of their discoveries could easily be communicated to a wider public if they could only contrive to be a little less fastidious and a little more human.

Not, I would insist, that one disbelieves in the idea of an intellectual aristocracy; the elect must lead. But to do so effectively they must not only be enlightened, but also be in natural sympathy with the masses. And the tendency of the average intellectual is in the opposite direction. He becomes exclusive, a devotee of a cult in which ordinary people are unable to participate. He finds it more and more difficult to communicate his ideas or enter into the outlook of less refined spirits, and this for the reason that he has made the mistake of confusing a certain technical method of dealing with human problems with the possession of a higher degree of illumination. His head has run ahead of his heart. And it is the heart alone which will enable a man to bridge the gulf between intellectual refinement and uninstructed simplicity. For the more deeply a thinker enters into that consciousness in which the head and the heart have become unified, the more likely is he to discover that his message can be conveyed in direct and easily assimilable terms. It is through his profound sense of union with his hearers that the true teacher is able to express his thoughts in a homely, yet forceful and accurate fashion. It is the heart alone which can convert intellectual into human statement.

The question has, however, a more important aspect. One cannot fail to observe that those ancient truths whose significance is at present being rediscovered by our intellectuals were originally enunciated by people who had not merely given them their theoretical assent, but who actually embodied them, and this to an outstanding degree. Men were not only presented with principles; the truth was radiated out to them through the medium of dynamic personalities. It reached them charged with the passion and faith of men and women who had not merely apprehended it intellectually, but were living that which they preached. Such people only formulated what they had actually experienced, what, indeed, they *were*. Thought was potent because it was one with being. The word was not only spoken, but made flesh.

Today, however, things are different. Our modern critics have *appropriated* the intellectual conclusions of these living, passionate people without paying the proper price for doing so. And the result is that their admonitions leave us unmoved. For we are not purely rational beings; we demand in the person addressing us a certain degree of eloquence, persuasiveness, and fire. And we are very well aware that these qualities do not become manifested unless he is speaking to us immediately out of his inner consciousness and not from his head alone.

5. Diagnosis versus Prescription

Nor is this all. We can hardly fail to observe that the truths which our intellectuals are engaged in impressing upon us are not exactly the truths which we most urgently need to know. For their chief contribution to modern thought lies in their recognition that certain problems must be fairly faced before any really constructive work can begin. They have defined the issues with commendable clarity, they have opened our eyes, told us in which direction we must look if we wish to gain a sight of the most vital factors in the case. *This* must be dealt with first; *that* recognized as being only of secondary importance; it is *here* that the fundamental issue lies. Before everything, it is needful that we should deepen our realization of such and such a truth, respond to a given call to action, set our feet on one particular way, submit ourselves to a certain type of discipline. Thus, we must face the fact that the essential problem before us today is that of discovering a modern substitute for grace (Mr Babbitt); or of developing 'disinterestedness' (Mr Lippmann); or of resisting the tyranny of Time (Mr Wyndham Lewis); or of realizing the significance of the metabiological (Mr Murry); or of acquiring a sense of the Whole (Mr Waldo Frank).

All this is to the good; clearly until the problem has been formulated nothing positive can be achieved. Yet at the same time we cannot help feeling, in the year 1931, that the early stages of the process of extricating us from our difficulties have now been traversed. We enjoy a fairly complete understanding of where the nineteenth century went wrong and of the tasks which lie immediately before us. And the result is that the exhortations which are addressed to us by our critics are beginning to fall a little monotonously upon our ears. We are becoming increasingly aware of the fact that there has been enough analysis, demonstration, and counselling. We are looking round for those people who will tell us what all this is to mean *in practice*. We are realizing that recognition is not the same thing as prescription, nor diagnosis the same thing as leadership. Both relate to the earliest and perhaps the least difficult stage of our emancipation. In other words, our critics are only dealing with ideals, with objectives, with *desiderata*. What we are now becoming exercised about is the mode of attaining them. The principles we want are principles of *action*.

We meet here with an aspect of the question which needs, I think, to be more courageously faced. One finds a writer like Mr Lippmann announcing with a certain satisfaction that the key to our difficulties lies in our failure to be 'disinterested' and 'mature'. And he points out that it was just this need for 'disinterestedness' and 'maturity' which was most heavily stressed by the teachers of 'high religion'. He omits, however, to refer to the fact that, according to these same teachers, the task of rendering oneself 'disinterested' was practically equivalent to the crucifixion of the ordinary human self. For when a person passes from merely *recognizing* the need for maturity to the stage of endeavouring to achieve it, he becomes involved immediately in a process of painful spiritual regeneration which sooner or later entails a modification of his whole being, physical, intellectual, and spiritual. In other words, although it does not need a great deal of perspicacity to perceive that maturity is the goal, with that realization the work has scarcely begun. For to be 'disinterested' means to kill, or die to, the personal self. And, as every enlightened spiritual teacher has always known, this is the most formidable undertaking which any man can attempt. Mr Lippmann, however, writes rather as if the formula which he has lit upon will by itself magically bring about the state of being which it characterizes.*

But the most important aspect of the matter is this. Directly it becomes a question for us, not of simply orientating ourselves properly, but of setting practically to work, the 'principles' which we need for our guidance become of a markedly different order. We require the assistance, not of the moralist, but of the spiritual teacher, the person who can aid us in the difficulties in which we immediately become involved on trying to embody our ideals. For we are now actively seeking to *be* something which we were not before, and this means that we are in need of the services of an expert in the Science of Being. We turn for help to those among us who are able to look with discernment into the deep places of the heart, that they may explain us to ourselves, penetrate to the root of our difficulties, show us what being 'mature' means in terms of actual life.

Until the modern age this highly responsible office was performed by the priest. Today it is performed by the psycho-analyst. With those who entertain the notion that we can afford to submit ourselves confidently to his ministrations I will not dispute here; I refer them to *The Learned Knife*. My point at the moment is that the vital issues do not lie exclusively even with such modern psychologists as are able to treat their patients on really

* The tendency to refer to the beginning of the road as if it were the end is very characteristic of our modern intellectuals. I find Mr Bertrand Russell writing that 'the supreme principle, both in politics and in private life, should be to promote all that is creative, and so to diminish the impulses and desires that centre round possession'. (*Principles of Social Reconstruction* (1916), p. 236) In the original Mr Russell has set the passage in italics, as much as to say that now that we have grasped this illuminating fact the worst is over. If only it were!

enlightened lines. Our modern intellectuals are also faced with the obligation of providing us with a spiritual evaluation of our experience. More and more, not only in the clinic, but in the wider field of literature, we are listening for the authoritative voices of those who can show us how to live aright.

We cannot but be sensible, however, that our intelligentsia are incapable of giving us the type of guidance which we require. For when it comes to passing from theory to practice, the only person who can really aid us is the man who has passed through a process of regeneration and acquired by direct experience an understanding of the deeper mysteries of the soul.

6. Ends and Beginnings

Finally, we have to consider the supremely important question of the relation of the thinker to his age.

It is evident enough that we are living in the midst of a period of transition, a period in which all our established and sanctified institutions are being swept away, while at the same time we are met with all manner of novel and bewildering manifestations which seem to presage the emergence of a new type of society. What the future holds for us no man dare confidently predict.

The attitudes which are adopted by critical minds in the face of the present world-situation may conveniently be divided into three main types: that of the conservative classicist, that of the disillusioned classicist, and that of the imaginative modernist.

Of the first we may say that he sees our hope of remedying the existing state of affairs to lie in a return to the Past. The present deplorable anarchy in values has for him only a negative significance; what is involved is a disastrous falling away from the 'standards of Western civilization '. The obligation laid upon us is that of living up to our heritage, of raising our culture to the level from which it has fallen. Such thinkers are primarily conscious of the *decline* which has set in relative to the achievements of the Past. And by stressing the need for preserving continuity with that Past they are implicitly affirming that the cultural cycle which began for us with the emergence of Greek civilization has not yet run its course. Such thinkers may, of course, despair of the future, but this is not the point; the point is that everything turns for them on whether or not we can return to the sound traditions of an earlier age.

The point of view of the disillusioned classicist is widely different. His attitude may be summed up in the phrase *tout est foutu.* The Spenglerian cycle is inexorably drawing to a close; all our traditional forms are dissolving before our eyes; we must abandon ourselves to fate. It is the end. On the face of it, it would seem that we are sliding down an inclined plane at the bottom of which lies annihilation. Whether or not there is, indeed, something new being born in the midst of the chaos it is impossible to say. The situation of the thinker who finds himself in such a Waste Land is tragic enough.

Finally, we have the imaginative modern. By the ' imaginative modern ' I mean the person whose strength lies in the fact that he is able to detect the modes in which the new life is beginning to manifest itself amidst the desolation which accompanies the death of the old order. He can in some measure decipher the characters in which the charter of the future age is written. He sees in the present chaos, not simply the element of decline and fall, but the earliest manifestations of something altogether new. Where the classicist can discover only disintegration and decay, he sees that disorder which in every sphere of being accompanies the process of rebirth. And he conceives our primary obligation to lie, not in orientating ourselves by the landmarks set up in the Past, but in apprehending as discerningly as possible the nature of the new life which is coming.

It is evident enough that the issue between the modernist and the classicist is far too deep to be bridged by rational discussion alone. The determining factor is in the blood. The evidence on which the modernist is basing his claims lies largely within his own being. He feels a new sap rising within him, he finds himself responding to a novel and vital rhythm, he is met on all sides with signs that the tide has begun to flow in a new direction. The classicist, on the other hand, is only able to detect the most abundant evidence of degradation and exhaustion. His eye is only for that which is in process of deterioration. And according to whether he is of the conservative or the disillusioned type he either strives to resist the disintegration or submits himself pessimistically to ineluctable destiny.

Now if it be really true that we are involved in nothing more than an episodal failure to maintain the old order, if the cycle has not yet run its full course—then both the disillusioned classicist and the modernist are failing to think in a realistic fashion, and the attitude of such uncompromising traditionalists as M. Maritain or Mr G. K. Chesterton is evidently fully justified. Our task is then that of setting to work to re-establish a Latin-Catholic civilization, and the sooner we devote ourselves to it the better. The modernist will then appear simply as one of those tiresome and undisciplined fanatics who invariably raise their voices during a period of disorder, and who make matters still worse by seeking to represent that disorder as the prelude to a new era. If, on the other hand, the modernist is right, then the position is exactly reversed, and we are confronted with that oft-repeated situation in which the conservative fails to recognize that a new cycle has begun, and sees in the disorder which attends regeneration nothing more than a failure to maintain established values.

As I say, what decides a man in choosing between these two interpretations is a condition of the blood. You either feel that a new cycle is beginning or you see around you only disorder and disaster. All argument is profitless; there remains only affirmation and counter-affirmation. Hence, I will merely record here my conviction that the modernist and the disillusioned classicist are in the right, and the conservative classicist in the wrong.

What follows? First of all, the conclusion that the attitude of our traditionalists is simply *irrelevant* to the modern situation. One can, of course, readily sympathize with their point of view. They are highly conscientious people, and deeply concerned regarding the present state of our civilization. On all sides they are met with disorder, with moral laxity, with the vulgarity which attends the triumph of democracy, with the disregard of all established norms. They are confronted with what appears to be complete chaos, and they can think of nothing better than to make a stand for traditional principles, to reaffirm the beliefs which were once so potent in the past, to recall us to the wisdom of the ancients. Many of the most intelligent of them, seized with fear at the prospects which are opening before them, are led to take refuge in the great Roman Catholic Church, which seems to them to be the only stable object remaining in the midst of the flux.

To those, however, who regard the existing situation as a major turning point in history, this attempt to return to the past presents itself as completely misdirected. It is utterly inappropriate to the point which we have reached in the cycle. There is a stage in the development of a culture when we need more than anything the services of those minds which excel in traditional wisdom, which are sensitive to precedents, which are imbued with a deep respect for authority, which are able to apply to the present the rich experience of the past. But this happens in the Autumn, when the harvest is being gathered in. And today it is only early Spring, when the qualities of which we are in need are far more those of intuition and faith. The people who will be significant in this age are the people who are endowed with the prophetic sense, the people who can orientate themselves to the potential rather than to the established. The first duty of the intellectual leader at the present time is to make a bold act of faith and dismiss from his mind all precedents, traditions, and accepted principles, and, leaving his sophisticated mind behind him, give himself up without fear or restraint to the spirit of the age. His primary duty is not to organize and codify, but to respond, to listen with humbleness and attention that he may catch the rhythm of the new life. As Mr Frank has so finely said, 'We must accept our chaos'.

And here, again, we become involved with the factor of Religion. For no merely *intellectual* person is capable of thus reading the signs of the times; that must be plainly understood. Nothing, indeed, could be more profitless and misleading than the 'brilliant forecasts', the 'anticipations', and the 'prophecies' which are indulged in by our intelligentsia in this connexion. For they are based almost entirely on calculation, on artful deductions from that which is already apparent to the eye. They are, therefore, of inconsiderable significance. And the reason is, quite simply, that the art of divination can only be practised with effect by those who have been spiritually quickened. In order to become discriminatingly modern the man must begin by deepening his being: he must become truly harmonized with the creative processes which are invisibly at work beneath the surface chaos. And to do this he needs, let us boldly affirm, to purify and humble himself to an extreme degree.

7. The Foundation of Insight

I have now indicated some of the more obvious ways in which our modern intelligentsia tend to disappoint us. And I have suggested also that the cause of their failure is to be sought in the fact that the discipline to which they have submitted themselves is excessively intellectual in type.

I cannot but feel that we are here confronted with a problem which is destined to cause us no little embarrassment in the near future. It is becoming increasingly apparent to us that the root of all our material difficulties is an incapacity to deal with the great spiritual issues which underlie all others. Yet at the same time we have lost faith in the religion of our forefathers. The consequence is that, as I have already pointed out, our intellectuals have taken over the function once exercised by the priesthood.

Now although the priests may have entertained all sorts of ideas which the modern man finds himself impelled to reject, there is this at least to be said for them. Following an agelong tradition, they acted on the assumption that the deeper laws of life were only to be understood at the cost of observing certain very stringent conditions. They did not consider themselves qualified to guide the destinies of the race unless they submitted themselves to a severe type of discipline. They accepted the principle that insight was the fruit of frugality, meditation, and prayer. They believed—the best of them—that the science of spiritual things was something apart from the other sciences and called for a special type of training. This both in the East and the West.

This is not the 'modern' belief. The modern belief is that all problems exist on the same level, that their solution is primarily a matter of intelligence and education, that the same kind of attitude—that of the alert, clear-headed, highly critical, and detached observer—is equally appropriate to every field of research.

Is this a view of the matter with which we can afford to remain satisfied? Is there no connexion between the fact that on the one hand our intellectual life has today become almost completely secularized and the fact that on the other our ideas on the subject of values are in a state of chaos? Manifestly there is. It is difficult to avoid concluding that what is primarily the matter with our intelligentsia is that they are endeavouring to solve our deeper problems in terms of thought rather than in terms of Being, that they are trying to secure their vision on unduly easy terms.

'If we are drifting back to barbarism', writes Professor Zimmern in his *Learning and Leadership*, 'the root of the evil is not political, but intellectual'. But he has elsewhere made plain that this is not the final truth about the matter; the root of the evil is *moral*. Moral because in the end the quality of the understanding depends upon the condition of the spirit. And that, if we are going to take a thoroughly realistic view of the question, is the point to be attacked first. The rest will follow; there is nothing the matter with our intellects, regarded as technical instruments for research.

Any exploration of the possibilities which are offered to our intellectuals in the way of spiritual catharsis would be out of place in these pages. But it is perhaps worth while to suggest that we moderns will not be able to discover any valuable principles relating to this question which have not already received the endorsement of discriminating minds in the past. Simplicity of life, the discipline of the will and the emotions, meditation, preoccupation with those things which belong to eternity rather than to time—the list is familiar enough.

One might add, however, that properly it should include prayer. For elevated states of mind are not to be attained to without a preliminary process of preparation. Describe the situation, if you will, by saying that a condition of slight auto-hypnosis must be induced. Now among the manifold means of bringing that hypnosis about the most potent, perhaps, is that of prayer: the individual opens his heart to God, and there results, as is well known, a heightening of the perceptions and a notable liberation of psychic energy. Through the fact that he has dedicated himself to Something which he believes to be transcendental in wisdom, love, and power, the man's energies are concentrated, purified, and reinforced.

Unfortunately, however, the modern intellectual does not happen to believe in God. Or, at the best, his God is something of the order of a bit of space-time, or a nisus towards perfection, communion with whom is hardly likely to prove a particularly invigorating affair. And the consequence is that, even if we are disposed to 'explain' religious worship in terms of purely subjective psychological processes, it remains true that through the decline of his faith he is deprived of an extremely potent stimulus —a stimulus which is at any rate indisputably more powerful than the coffee and the cigarettes for which he is accustomed to reach out in the search for inspiration. And to that degree he is at a disadvantage compared with his predecessors in an earlier age.

But for the moment we will leave the question of God out of account. I limit myself here to the contention that the primary problem before us if we wish to extract ourselves from our difficulties is not so much that of disciplining the mind as that of disciplining that something within ourselves which determines the character of its activity. And this is equivalent again to saying that it is to our hearts rather than to our heads that our attention should at the present time first be directed. We must be spiritually quickened before anything really fundamental can be accomplished. As Mr Middleton Murry has written, 'The need of a new asceticism is upon us'.

Only rarely do we come across a critic who devotes himself with any seriousness to trying to *be* what he teaches. That is why the case of Mr Waldo Frank presents such singular interest. For we last catch sight of him, at the end of his *Rediscovery of America*, actively striving by certain practical exercises to realize in his own person that 'sense of the Whole' to which he attaches such significance. I say this quite apart from the question of the value which may inhere in his theories and disciplines. The point is that his *attitude* is the right one. The words of such a man may one day conceivably be with power; he will be able to speak directly to us out of his interior experience. And it may not be long before it is only to this type of person that we shall feel disposed to listen.

CHAPTER IV

THE NEW HUMANISM

In considering, in this chapter, the question of moral behaviour we come at last face to face with the central issue. The problem before us is to decide whether men and women can derive adequate inspiration and support from ethical principles alone, or whether they are not driven in the end to transcend this level of apprehension and realize the Good in that more interior and immediate fashion which we associate with the religious experience. In pursuing our enquiries we shall be obliged to examine the theories of our modern humanists and compare them as carefully as possible with those of the exponents of the New Romanticism. And, as a result of this confrontation, we may perhaps attain to an insight into the matter which neither of the two schools can severally be deemed to possess.

Any examination of the principles of Humanism which is undertaken in the year 1931 resolves itself naturally into an analysis of the ideas of that group of American critics who, under the distinguished leadership of Professor Irving Babbitt, are at present engaged in propagating the doctrines of the New Humanism. And since, again, no one of his followers would appear to have made any notable advance beyond the point reached originally by Mr Babbitt, I propose to confine my attention here to the extremely able exposition of his case which is to be found in his two latest volumes, *Rousseau and Romanticism* (1919) and *Democracy and Leadership* (1924).* This is, I think, a perfectly safe procedure. For it may truly be said of Mr Babbitt that he is a representative figure. Modern Humanism stands or falls according to whether or not his theories can be shown to be valid. Its whole

* Quoted hereafter as *R. and R.* and *D. and L.*

strength and weakness stand revealed in his pages, which express, not simply the attitude of one man, but that of a definite type of mind. To deal with his work is to touch the centre of the whole problem.

1. The Inner Check

The point of departure of his philosophy is the classical conception of man as a being who is at war with himself. Man's higher ethical will finds itself in continual conflict with his lower nature, which is a slave to limitless expansive desire:

Like all the great Greeks, Aristotle recognizes that man is the creature of two laws: he has an ordinary or natural self of impulse and desire and a human self that is known practically as a power of control over impulse and desire. If man is to become human he must not let impulse and desire run wild, but must oppose to everything excessive in his ordinary self, whether in thought or deed or emotion, the law of measure. This insistence on restraint and proportion is rightly taken to be of the essence not merely of the Greek spirit, but of the classical spirit in general. (*R. and R.* 16)

The discipline which the individual imposes upon his baser propensities takes the form of the famous 'inner check':

As against the expansionists of every kind, I do not hesitate to affirm that what is specifically human in man and ultimately divine is a certain quality of will, a will that is felt in its relation to his ordinary self as a will to refrain. (*D. and L.* 6)

The spiritual positivist then will start from a fact of immediate perception—from the presence namely in the breast of a principle of vital control (*frein vital*), and he will measure his spiritual strenuousness or spiritual sloth by the degree to which he exercises, or fails to exercise, this power. (*R. and R.* 153)

The result of this operation of the *frein vital* is that the man achieves moderation and sobriety, mediates between extremes, balances the centrifugal and centripetal elements in his being:

> All the furies lie in wait for the man who overextends himself. He is ripening for Nemesis. 'Nothing too much'. 'Think as a mortal'. 'The half is better than the whole'. In his attitude towards man's expansive self the Greek as a rule stands for mediation, and not like the more austere Christian for renunciation. (*R. and R.* 253)

But it is important to observe that Mr Babbitt's standpoint differs in two important respects from that of the pure Hellenist. He differs from him, first, in respect of the significance which he attaches to the will:

> Anyone who wishes to recover the true dualism must begin by exalting the ethical will to the first place. Any attempt to give the primacy to 'reason' in any sense of the word will result in the loss of humility and lead to a revival, in some form, of the Stoical error. One must in this matter not only side with the Christian against the Stoic, but in general with the Asiatic against the European intellectual. (*D. and L.* 226)

And, in the second place, he assigns a particularly important function to the imagination:

> I come here to another distinctive feature of the type of humanism I am defending. I not only have more to say of will and less of reason than the humanist in the Græco-Roman tradition, but I also grant a most important rôle to imagination. (*D. and L.* 10)
>
> The centre of normal human experience that is to serve as a check on impulse (so far at least as it is something distinct from the mere convention of one's age and time) can be apprehended only with the aid of the imagination. (*R. and R.* 201)
>
> Pascal saw, rightly, that the balance of power in such a conflict between reason and impulse was held by the imagina-

tion, and that if reason lacked the support of insight the imagination would side with the expansive desires and reason would succumb. (*R. and R.* 178)

The process of orientating oneself to reality involves, in fact, the use of the will, the imagination, and the reason in conjunction:

It is only through the analytical head and its keen discriminations that the individualist can determine whether the unity and infinitude towards which his imagination is reaching . . . is real or merely chimerical. (*R. and R.* 167)

Finally, the individual, although he is enjoined to be resolutely 'experimental' in his attitude, is provided with certain standards which embody the wisdom attained to by men in the past, and which can assist him in the task of evaluating his own experience:

Having decided what is normal either for man or some particular class of men, the classicist takes this normal 'nature' for his model and proceeds to imitate it. Whatever accords with the model he pronounces natural or probable, whatever, on the other hand, departs too far from what he conceives to be the normal type or the normal sequence of cause and effect, he holds to be 'improbable' and unnatural or even, if it attains an extreme of abnormality, 'monstrous'. (*R. and R.* 16)

The very heart of the classical message, one cannot repeat too often, is that one should aim first of all not to be original, but to be human, and that to be human one needs to look up to a sound model and imitate it. (*R. and R.* 64)

A man needs to look, not down, but up to standards set so much above his ordinary self as to make him feel that he is himself spiritually the underdog. (*D. and L.* 257)

The more purely philosophical objections which can be brought against the system which Mr Babbitt builds up on this foundation have been marshalled already elsewhere by abler hands than mine.* It is by no means easy to understand the nature of the ideal which emerges when the conclusions of 'the best minds' throughout the ages have been collected together; for one thing, the principle of selection is far from clear. And in any case, as Mr Eliot justly points out, 'Boil down Horace, the Elgin Marbles, St Francis, and Goethe, and the result will be pretty thin soup'. Nor is it apparent how exactly the individual is to contrive to be 'experimental' and traditional at the same time. And, lastly, Mr Babbitt's use of the term 'civilization' offers serious difficulties.

But these questions I will here leave aside. My concern in this essay is solely with the relationship between Humanism and Religion.

2. Humanism and Religion

The first point that claims our attention is that the problem is one which has not failed to present itself to Mr Babbitt himself with considerable insistence. In his *Rousseau and Romanticism* he writes in the following terms:

> The preference I have expressed for a positive and critical humanism I wish to be regarded as very tentative. In the dark situation that is growing up in the Occident, all genuine humanism and religion, whether on a traditional or a critical basis, should be welcome. I have pointed out that traditional humanism and religion conflict in certain respects, that it is difficult to combine the imitation of Horace with the imitation of Christ. This problem does not disappear entirely when humanism and religion are dealt with critically, and is indeed one of the most obscure that the thinker has to face. The honest thinker, whatever his own preference, must

* See particularly Mr Eliot's essays, 'The Humanism of Irving Babbitt' (in *For Lancelot Andrewes*), and 'Second Thoughts on Humanism' (*The New Adelphi*, August, 1929).

begin by admitting that, though religion can get along without humanism, humanism cannot get along without religion. (*R. and R.* 379)

One may observe in passing that very much the same attitude is displayed by the other veteran leader of the humanistic movement in America, Professor Paul E. More. In the course of an article in the *American Bookman* for March, 1930, he frankly expresses the most serious doubts regarding the adequacy of a purely humanistic philosophy:

The high value of being a man—is that *telos* attainable, is it even approachable, without religion? The question disquiets me as a humanist. . . . Will not the humanist, unless he adds to his creed the faith and hope of religion, find himself at the last, despite his protests, dragged back into the camp of the naturalist?

Returning to Mr Babbitt, we find that, in spite of his misgivings, he has definitely chosen to take his stand upon a humanistic philosophy. And this for the following reasons:

I . . . may give at least one reason here for inclining to the humanistic solution. I have been struck in my study of the past by the endless self-deception to which man is subject when he tries to pass too abruptly from the naturalistic to the religious level. The world, it is hard to avoid concluding, would have been a better place if more persons had made sure they were human before setting out to be superhuman; and this consideration would seem to apply with special force to a generation like the present that is wallowing in the trough of naturalism. (*R. and R.* xx)

It might be well, therefore, for us to undertake something more within our capacity than religion. In general, for one person who has even an inkling of the nature of a genuinely religious working and of the strenuous peace at which religion aims, at least a hundred persons can be found who can grasp to some extent the type of work that has its fruition in the mediatory or humanistic virtues. (*D. and L.* 195)

And again:

I am concerned, in other words, less with the meditation in which true religion always culminates, than in (with?) the mediation or observance of the law of measure that should govern man in his secular relations. (*D. and L.* 6) I hold that at the heart of genuine Christianity are certain truths which have already once saved Western civilization and, judiciously employed, may save it again. (22) What is needed just now is a revival of the ethical will on the secular level, where it is felt as a will to justice, rather than on the religious level, where it is felt as a will to peace. (197) The humanist would not go beyond disciplining the 'lusts' of the natural man to the law of measure. (230)

The first comment that one is impelled to make in considering the above passages is that they reveal a singular lack of penetration into the more interior aspects of our moral experience. Mr Babbitt writes very nearly as if the individual was in a position to make a cool and dispassionate choice between being moral and being religious. Yet it should surely be plain that the effect of any religious experience that is authentic is that of *compelling* one to live on a mystical rather than on an ethical basis. The man is possessed by something infinitely more powerful than himself. He feels within a new and disturbing life, finds himself in an unfamiliar realm of being in which alone he can thenceforward exist without distress. The notion that after having undergone such an expansion of consciousness he can elect to restrict his idealistic efforts to exercising the humanistic virtues is simply untenable. The only type of religion which can be set aside in this deliberate fashion is the religion which is too anæmic to be worthy of the name. The alternatives offered us are unreal. The humanist cannot be properly said to reject a possibility which has never become actual for him; and when religion becomes a fact of experience such rejection is out of the question.

But can we in any case agree that for one person who can understand the principles of religion there are a hundred who can understand those of Humanism? One suspects that Mr Babbitt has here been led astray by his rationalistic preference for the clear-cut and the intelligible. Obviously, the number of people who can comprehend the meaning of self-control, sobriety, discretion, and the like is extremely large; no one would deny that the teachings of a purely secular morality are easy enough to assimilate—though, doubtless, they are hard enough to act upon. Obviously, again, the significance of religion in its most lofty and interior aspects is appreciated by the elect alone. But it remains true that religion, in one form or another, has always been congenial to the minds of the vast mass of mankind—for the good reason that it involves an appeal to the imagination, which Humanism very distinctly does not. Religion by its rites and ceremonies, by its disciplines and scriptures, brings the truths of morality home to the understanding of us all. Our instincts and senses are very properly brought into relation with our ethical aspirations and perceptions. The religious attitude is pre-eminently the *natural* attitude, and always will be.

The humanist, on the contrary, has always been a comparatively isolated figure. It is true that there are among us those who are only capable of conceiving the problem of spiritual discipline in purely ethical terms. And for such people the way of life indicated above may well prove the best. But they are certainly *not* 'representative' human beings. On the contrary, they strike one as being, in the Aristotelian sense of the term, extremely 'improbable'. Improbable because, although their concern with the need for the *frein vital* would seem to indicate that they share the passions of the rest of mankind (and yet even of this fact one is inclined to be doubtful; for surely no truly passionate person would rest content with mere self-restraint!), they are isolated from them by reason of their inordinate insensitiveness to the mystery of life.

The superior insight of Religion, on the contrary, lies in the fact that it directs the attention immediately to that central core of being in which our virtues have their source, that it concerns itself with that which provides the key to the whole position, and sets before us the supreme aim of changing ourselves at the roots—incidentally bringing our emotions into play in a way which is otherwise impossible. Hence that which for Humanism is primary is for Religion subsidiary—as is admirably brought out in the passage from Sir Thomas Browne quoted by Mr McEachran in his *Civilized Man*:

> I give no alms only to satisfy the hunger of my brother, but to fulfil and accomplish the Will and Command of my God; I draw not my purse for his sake that demands it, but His that enjoined it; I relieve no man upon the Rhetorick of his miseries, nor to content mine own commiserating disposition.

The efflorescence of the humanistic virtues is, then, a manifestation of a secondary order. But as to how far our classical humanists are prepared to recognize the fact one is not altogether clear. Mr Babbitt, as we have seen, has not rejected the religious experience altogether unconditionally; there are certain truths which may be 'judiciously employed'. Mr McEachran, on the other hand, seems to go farther. Nevertheless, in his valuable essay, he is concerned to advance the view that man expresses himself typically by the exercise of the ethical will. He certainly believes that that will must be subordinated to another which is higher. But he does not make it very clear (to me, at least) how far he holds that man can effect that subordination without entering into a consciousness which is of a different order from the purely ethical consciousness.

This is a momentous question, and it is not out of place to recall here the fact that the verdict of history is rather decisively in favour of the conclusion that Humanism cannot, indeed, 'do without Religion'. The classical age of Greece concluded, as everybody knows, with a 'failure of nerve': men came to realize that the exercise of the humanistic virtues was only to be ensured if they attained first of all to a more intimate association with the Good than that provided for them by philosophy. They became alive to the significance of such conceptions as those of sin, rebirth, atonement, expiation, salvation, reconciliation—ideas which could only have meaning to a consciousness which had passed through a crisis of major importance. The humanist, on the contrary, is still concerning himself with issues which are not really central and vital.

The whole history of man's attempts to deal with the moral problem reveals very clearly his dependence upon his physical senses on the one hand and upon his theorizing intelligence on the other. That experience of inward identification with the Good which is known to the true mystic is for the mass of men too subtle and impalpable to be real. They are driven to resort to some form of exteriorization. Goodness must be envisaged in terms of its outworkings, of its concrete and tangible manifestations. And this involves a danger, to which it is only too easy to succumb, of concentrating inordinately upon derivative rather than upon primary problems.

The more obvious form of this extraversion is that which is represented by the humanitarian ideal of performing actions which are visibly 'constructive' and useful. The objective must be concrete, and more or less immediately attainable. The thinker of this school calls upon us before everything to act 'realistically', to bring about definite and beneficial changes in the material strucure of society. Mr Wells's 'open conspirator', with his passion for practical politics and scientific measures, is typical of this tendency.

Heaven forbid that one should be guilty of failing to recognize the value of such an attitude to the moral problem! Mr Wells, like everybody else who is genuinely concerned regarding the distress of our existing civilization, has our real respect. But one must yet stand firm in maintaining (in perfect accord here with the humanist) that the attitude is superficial—simply because it fails to take account of what is finally implied in setting about such a task. As generations of such optimistic extraverts have discovered to their chagrin, man cannot in the end draw his inspiration from contemplating the material ends which he is seeking to realize. The basis of effective activity on the material plane is an internal anchorage to something within which is raised above the level of the fluctuating and fugitive. It is because Mr Wells has never properly brought himself to face this fact that his splendid generosity and idealism have never been directed into truly creative channels.

And even when the emphasis has been shifted from the sphere of material activity to that of moral behaviour, the tendency towards exteriorization still makes itself manifest. There are certain modern psychologists—the school of Adler is typical in this respect—who exhort us before everything to cultivate such qualities as sympathy, kindliness, sociability. They exercise on the whole a valuable and salutary influence. Yet with all our appreciation of their idealism we cannot but perceive that the root of the matter really lies much deeper. For it is evident that the characteristics on which they lay such stress are only the outcome of a certain interior condition which, once it is properly established, will ensure their appearance. Kindliness does not come primarily from being kind; it comes from attaining to a state of which kindliness is one of the exterior manifestations. This is not to say that a person who deliberately sets about to be courteous, appreciative, and unselfish, will not reap a valuable harvest. But it remains true that, apart from the fact that he is thereby seriously exposed to the danger of becoming self-righteous, he is not dealing with the problem in its fundamental aspect. Our radical task is to turn inwards and change ourselves; the rest will follow. We cannot safely afford to regard as ends what should rightly be conceived of as consequences.

Now, when we turn once more to the humanists, we cannot but be conscious of the fact that they yield to the same tendency to extraversion, although that extraversion is effected this time on the intellectual rather than the material plane. By this I mean that they identify themselves with the Good as it is reflected in the mental consciousness in terms of principles, axioms, and norms. The nature of the situation is very exactly conveyed by the words of William James (otherwise, by the way, something very much more than a humanist) when, in writing about his personal faith, he admitted that 'the Divine, for my *active* life, is limited to abstract concepts which, as ideals, interest and determine me, but do so but faintly, in comparison with what a feeling of God might effect, if I had one'. That even the most mystical of us are dependent upon intellectual formulations goes, of course, without saying; the mind, no less than the senses, must be pressed into the service of morality. What I would urge in regard to the classicist, however, is that he is conditioned unduly by this obligation. His ethical attitude is, I admit, more fundamental than that of the thinker who concentrates primarily upon our actual behaviour in the world, for he takes his stand upon something more interior and abstract. His object is to associate himself with a principle (the moral law) which is thought of as being somehow inherent in Reality. His point of departure is not the phenomenal universe, but that changeless and enduring realm of being which we apprehend within. He is independent of the flux. Even though all the works of man pass away, justice is eternal.

Yet it remains true that he is disastrously limited by his intellectualism. He is still living 'under the law'. His concern is still, before everything, with the exercise of a certain range of virtues. He has not yet attained to that interior freedom which guarantees their appearance. He remains circumspect, isolated, self-regarding, lonely, aligned with the Good rather than identified with it. He has yet to attain to that liberating realization which is the fruit of all true religious illumination: the realization that that within himself which is striving to manifest virtue is consubstantial with Something other than himself—*quelquechose en moi qui soit plus moi-même que moi*—and that by courageously relinquishing his exacerbated self-consciousness and merging into that Something he can attain to release, tranquillity, and joy.

3. The Problem of Humility

One thing, however, is plain. The individual who is impelled to impose a check upon his naturalistic self, but who is not at the same time prepared to make this act of subordination to a Will that is higher than his own, is treading an extremely perilous path. And this Mr Babbitt perfectly well knows—even though, in spite of this realization, he has chosen to take his stand on Humanism alone. Consider the following remarks:

If anyone wishes to be a true modern, if he refuses, in other words, to submit to authority merely as such, he is confronted with a serious problem: it is plainly not easy to be at once humble and self-reliant. (*D. and L.* 166) But it will not be found easy to preserve humility and at the same time to grant, after the fashion of Greek philosophy, the primacy to mind. (173) Humanism must . . . like religion, subordinate intellect to the ethical will and so put its ultimate emphasis on humility. In this matter of humility the Western humanist has something to learn, as I have already hinted, from Confucian China. (195) Nothing will avail short of humility. Humility, as Burke saw, is the ultimate root of the justice that should prevail in the secular order, as well as of the virtues that are specifically religious. (258)

Further:

One comes to feel that the great religious teachers may be right after all in their insistence that man needs to subordinate himself to some higher will; above all, that his intellect should recognize some such control. (*D. and L.* 182) The problem would seem to be to recover the truths of grace in some individualistic form. (194) It can be shown that the doctrine of grace was the keystone of the whole edifice of European society in its medieval form. It is not as clear as one might wish that European civilization can survive the collapse of this doctrine. In any case, the problem for the individualist who believes that it is not enough to be self-reliant, but that one should also be humble, is to discover some equivalent for grace. (183)

Now, one cannot but feel that in this matter the humanist is presented with a very definite dilemma. For he must either be prepared to undergo a profound change of consciousness, and thereby transcend the humanistic plane altogether, or he must remain for ever exposed to the danger of becoming the victim of an arrogant and self-regarding egotism. Either the individual self must die and be reborn in the One, or it must pay the penalty for failing to pass beyond its own limits. Submission to a higher Will entails in the last resort the annihilation of one's egoistic centre: henceforward it is upon Something other than, and yet within, ourselves that we must depend. And to the extent that we achieve this union between the lesser and the greater I AM, we are saved from arrogance by realizing that although our vices are our own our virtues are not. Here alone lies safety.

'It is plainly not easy to be at once humble and self-reliant'. And it is, I hope, not unkind to discover a certain significance in the fact that the most able exponent of the doctrines of the new humanists is himself a remarkably self-reliant person, and at the same time not noticeably distinguished for the humbleness of his outlook. The whole tone of his writing is, in fact, peculiarly overbearing and uncompromising, at times almost intolerably arrogant. And though we thoroughly appreciate the play of his caustic wit and his exceptional power of trenchant and ironical statement, we cannot fail to perceive also that there is a certain connexion between the inner spirit of his teachings and the manner in which he enunciates them.

I am not, of course, suggesting that Humanism and humanity can never be found in association. But I do insist on the fact that the basis of the whole humanistic attitude is an obstinate and deep-seated egoism which is only reinforced by the individual's efforts to transcend it. For, by a fatal necessity, the more he concentrates his energies on the task of becoming more altruistic and disciplined, the more does he exacerbate the very individuality which he is so strenuously endeavouring to chasten. As Mr Fausset has admirably phrased it in his *Proving of Psyche*:

> The champions both of *self*-expression and *self*-control remain egotists because they falsely assert themselves against life. . . . The very opposition between reason and passion betrays a false self-centredness which must be resolved in imagination. . . . The conscience which sits in judgment and inhibits impulse is fallacious because it is self-engrossed.

. . . Mr Babbitt does not see that so long as the mind of man plays the part of Menelaus it will be betrayed by the senses which it fears and thinks to master, that it will not find truth and goodness in beauty, because its relation to beauty will be one of latent enmity. . . . For if the instincts are repressed instead of being expressively directed they become, just as when they are indulged, the satanic forces which Mr Babbitt regards them.

This is the root of the whole matter. The man who is devoting his powers to perfecting his own self inevitably becomes a victim of egoism. And, as Mr Babbitt himself has again recognized, he can only be saved from such an egoism by the operation of that influence to which we formerly gave the name of grace. In other words, he must attain to a condition in which the innermost centre of his being is subordinated to something above himself. Then only will he really be at peace.

It is at this point that the significance of the romantic attitude to the moral problem becomes apparent. For it is of the essence of the romantic that he is 'expansive', that he passes beyond the confines of his own being by merging himself in a wider unity. When this process takes place on the higher, rather than on the naturalistic, level, when, that is to say, he is able in this fashion to realize the true rather than the false infinite, the result is a transcendence of the egoistic plane. He 'dies' to his own self and becomes united with the Whole. Let me quote again from Mr Fausset's illuminating pages:

Mr Babbitt's . . . criticism of Romanticism, like his ideal of 'humanism', is inadequate, because it unduly prescribes both the needs and the potencies of human nature, because it refuses to recognize how urgent has grown man's hunger for a deeper mode of being, for a unity, demonstrated as attainable by the greatest poetry, in which the mind no longer stands in a merely judicial relation to the heart. . . . It is by opposing his will to his desires that the individual becomes conscious of himself. But he cannot complete himself until he has reconciled his will with desires that rise in him from a deeper source, from the original unquenchable fount of life. . . . A world which possessed the Gospels, though still Pagan in conduct, has differed from the pre-Christian world, through its realization, however dim, that the state of opposition, which seemed inevitable to the advance from the primitive to the conscious, is not final and irremediable, but a condition of growth towards a truer unity. It was because Paganism lacked this conception that even its great poets and moral philosophers are, by comparison with the poets and saints who have assimilated Jesus' teaching, negative. Their morality was not perfected in the imagination, which Joubert named 'the eye of the soul'. They could not conceive a state in which morality ceased to be a discipline and became an expressive joy. . . .

And again:

And the discovery of the true Romantic is just the new centre of being which Mr Babbitt denies. It is a personal, but no longer a selfish centre, because the individual has submitted himself, not blindly to the flux, but with 'the open eye of imagination', with all that implies of active and discriminating intelligence, to the creative will of life. Thereby he has become a true centre of life, an organic being in whose consciousness the unconscious takes form and meaning.

I may observe here that not only the traditional insight of religion, but all the most valuable teachings in modern psychology, go to discredit Mr Babbitt's treatment of the ethical problem. There is no tranquillity for the individual until the discords within his being have been resolved, his passions properly sublimated. The self must be unified. Admittedly the achievement of that unification is the privilege of a few, and for the majority of men a rather distant possibility. And it is true also that until integrity has been attained it is better for a man to control his passions than to yield to them. But that compromise should be recognized for what it is—a temporary and unsatisfactory expedient. The fact remains that if we wish to live creatively we must undertake something more fundamental than merely checking our lower impulses. The end of the road is not repression, but transmutation. In our present unhappy condition we are divided beings, but the obligation laid upon us is that of transforming this dualism into a unity. Until we are regenerated and not merely controlled our condition must necessarily be one of impotence and distress.

4. The Transcendence of Morality

Psychic health is, then, the product, not of repression, but of sublimation. The man is only whole when his instincts, so far from being merely held in check, are dedicated to the service of something beyond himself. And where the classicist fails is in neglecting to give this fact due weight.

Not that Mr Babbitt has not recognized its significance. He admits freely that the man who has become truly religious is in some peculiar sense beyond the law:

> Not even Aristotle himself would maintain that the law of measure applies to saintliness, and in general to the religious realm. The saint, in so far as he is saintly, has undergone conversion, has in the literal sense of the word faced around and is looking in an entirely different direction from that to which the warnings 'nothing too much' and 'think as a mortal' apply. (*R. and R.* 222)

And he quotes the observation of Aristotle (*Eth. Nic.* 1177b) that

> we should not give heed to those who bid one think as a mortal, but so far as we can we should make ourselves immortal and do all with a view to a life in accord with the best Principle in us. (*R. and R.* 253)

But in practice he prefers to take the other path, and enjoins upon us that we should remain within the limits of the human. The ideal which he sets before us is therefore strictly limited. It is assumed that as a result of imposing a check upon our expansive desires we shall merely become more 'sober', more 'probable', more fundamentally sane. Such discipline will have the effect of drawing us back into our natural bounds, of preventing us from being guilty of lack of balance or 'excess'. We shall remain properly 'representative', and be kept out of mischief.

We find a similar attitude displayed by Mr McEachran. He writes, for example, that 'the civilized man is nothing more or less in the last analysis than the hero of tragedy'. And what impresses him particularly in the life and death of Jesus is the supreme manifestation of will that is involved. To look at the question from this point of view is, in one sense, sound enough. But at the same time it is evident that Mr McEachran, like Mr Babbitt, is considering the situation to an excessive degree as it appears when regarded from *without*. The attitude of the righteous man then seems to be largely passive. He is engaged all the time in resisting, in holding back, in preserving his integrity, in rising above his fate. But if on the other hand we consider his condition instead from *within* we perceive that what presents itself to the classical observer as being a denial of the natural is really only the negative aspect of an inward realization of the Divine. His repudiation of evil and falsehood is incidental to a tremendous interior experience of Reality. To describe his conduct only from the point of view of his denials and abstentions is seriously to misrepresent its character.

It is precisely this conception of the consequences of self-discipline which the romantic and the mystic will most resolutely dispute. They will agree unreservedly that the submission to limitation is the condition of all true freedom and creativeness. But they will insist no less definitely that when that submission is complete the result must inevitably be something infinitely more potent and intoxicating than decorum and proportion. And this for the significant reason that in the purely classical conception of the situation there is left out of account one highly important factor—the factor of emotion.

Read the pages of Mr Babbitt and you will find that the whole force of his eloquence is directed upon the need to restrain the expansion of the spirit on the naturalistic plane. On this dangerous and disorderly tendency we must impose the salutary check of the *frein vital*. We agree. But what we go on to enquire is: In what form does this emotional outpouring reappear in the properly disciplined individual? What substitute does Mr Babbitt provide for that delirious, if ill-advised, fusion with Nature in which the Rousseauistic phantast is so prone to indulge?

If we are informed that it reappears only in the form of a wise submissiveness to Fate, a resigned acceptance of the fact of one's mortality, a display of the purely negative virtues, then we can only reply quite bluntly that the answer will not satisfy us at all. For to create, as Mr Babbitt has done, a false opposition between will and passion is to misconceive the workings of the psychic organism in the grossest possible fashion. The true opposition can only be between elevated passion on the one hand and less elevated passion on the other. It is clearly the function of the will, working in co-operation with the reason and the imagination, not simply to dam up the flow of passion, but to direct it into creative channels. The alternative is, in fact, a neurosis.

Mr Babbitt has expressed himself at great length and with remarkable penetration on the subject of the dangers attending a response to the false infinite of personal desire. And that response involves, not only a great liberation of emotion, but also a dissipation, in a wrongful sense, of the egocentric self. Is it not plain that when the individual has learned to respond to the *true* infinite the same elements of emotion and self-transcendence will again come into play on a higher level? Must not the equivalent of a false ecstasy (false because doomed to culminate in a revulsion of feeling) be a true ecstasy?

Of course it must! And the decisive indication of the failure of the humanistic thinker to penetrate to the root of this particular problem lies just in the fact that his ideal is a person who has achieved by his prodigious self-discipline nothing but an inoffensive and uninteresting integrity. For this simply serves to show that that discipline, so far from being excessive, *has not been carried far enough*. This is the great discovery of mystical religion and the key to its superior and perennial appeal. For what the mystic asserts is, in a word, that to slay the old Adam is *ipso facto* to realize God. To the extent, that is to say, that you really subdue the baser passions you necessarily liberate within yourself the exuberant divine. Check the propensities of the animal soul and you at once pass into a wider, a more intense, and a more exultant consciousness. Beyond the circumscribed existence of the unregenerated individual there lies, waiting to be realized, not the relatively insipid serenity of Humanism, but positive exhilaration and delight. The life of the spirit is essentially one of inner joy.

The classical 'balance', on the contrary, is achieved by stopping halfway. The 'middle path' passes through a no-man's land which lies between two arbitrarily separated worlds. What we are confronted with is the expression of a process which has not been carried to its proper conclusion. It involves an impoverished neutrality, a state in which the world has been transcended without being regained, a death which has not been crowned by rebirth. It was for a good reason that Dante consigned the humanist to the Limbo of his Inferno. For he signalized thereby the fact that the alternative to existence on the purely biological level is *not* the moderation and temperance of the thoroughly controlled individual, but the liberation of his impulses on a higher and more creative level. According to Eastern psychologists, the inevitable consequence of checking the downward flow of the vital principle on the plane of earthly desire is its rising along the spinal column to awaken in the initiate vision, bliss, and spiritual power. Which statement, even if we are not disposed to regard it as being physiologically true, may at least serve us as an illuminating allegory.

5. Romanticism, True and False

But anything of the order of expansion, of movement away from the egoistic self, Mr Babbitt regards with the deepest distrust: it becomes for him synonymous with naturalistic self-indulgence, with a relapse to the plane of purely biological existence. He refuses to recognize, with Mr Fausset, 'a state in which morality ceases to be a discipline and becomes an expressive joy'. After taking care to remind us that the counsels of Socrates's 'voice' were always negative, never positive, he observes that

> perhaps the first discovery that anyone will make who wishes to be at once critical and enthusiastic is that in a genuinely spiritual enthusiasm the inner light and the inner check are practically identical. (*R. and R.* 258)

This is surely a questionable assertion. Although the most significant of the intimations of conscience are usually admonitions to abstain, the rule is by no means invariable. Need one recall the exhortation that rang in Augustine's ears to 'take and read, take and read'? And anyone who studies the pages of George Fox's *Journal* cannot fail to be impressed by the fact that the 'inner light' was continually impelling him, not only to hold back, but to venture forth in the most daring fashion. And what of the experience of the great Hebrew prophets? 'The word of the Lord came unto Jonah the son of Amittai, saying, Arise, go to Nineveh, that great city, and cry against it'.

The truth is that at the root of Mr Babbitt's desire to lay such weight on the negative aspect of intuition there lies a deep-seated, Puritanical fear of the emotions. He has failed to attain to that deeper consciousness in which the head and the heart are one. And the result is that *once he leaves the intellectual plane he has no centre left from which to control his experience*. In this simple fact we are, I believe, provided with a key to the whole character of his philosophy, and incidentally with a decisive indication of why that philosophy will not avail us. He is an intellectualist who is unwilling to face the ultimately inescapable obligation of putting his trust in a wisdom which is only to be acquired at the cost of transcending that plane on which the intellectualistic self is supreme.

In reading his writings we meet with indications of this fact at every point. In developing the argument of his *Rousseau and Romanticism*, for instance, he incidentally drops the remark that 'illusion is the element in which woman even more than man would seem to live and move and have her being. It is feminine and also romantic to prefer to a world of sharp definition a world of magic and suggestiveness'. I cannot help feeling that we are here confronted with one of those tell-tale little asides which so frequently serve to give a writer's whole case away. For in making this contemptuous and undeserved comment he has revealed to us the extent of the limitations under which his mind works. Every man who has any sense of spiritual truth is aware that woman is, if anything, far more 'realistic' in her outlook than man, because she responds instinctively to that element of 'vital novelty' in life to which the theorizing male tends to be blind. It lies deep in her nature that (if she has not become 'emancipated' in the wrong sense and thereby transmogrified into a creature that has lost the essential virtues of her sex while failing at the same time to acquire the virtues of the male) she should individualize the situation, do that which is called for by the uniqueness of the circumstances in which she finds herself.

It is just on account of this immediate reaction to the living moment that she irritates and bewilders the excessively masculine type, and is so hopelessly misunderstood by such systematically minded people as Mr Babbitt. For, as I have said, he is so constituted that he can only recognize right action when its theoretical basis is clearly evident to him. His attitude is that of the rationalist for whom 'a world of sharp definition' is the only one which is truly real. That which eludes classification and description and can only be apprehended by the imagination belongs for him to the realm of illusion. He is both disturbed and confused by spontaneity, because in dealing with its manifestations he is unable to make use of those formal, legalistic methods with which alone he is at home.

If, however, we wish to obtain a decisive indication of his deep-seated fear of the emotions we must turn to his treatment of the romantic problem. What do we discover? We discover that his analysis of the weaknesses inherent in the romantic outlook is nothing short of masterly; he has exposed the egoism, the naturalistic self-indulgence, the pseudo-idealism of the romantics with an unerring hand. And we are sincerely grateful to him for having executed such a distinguished piece of work: *Rousseau and Romanticism* remains one of the most remarkable contributions to criticism that have been made in this century. Yet at the same time we are bound to recognize that he exhibits a disastrous blindness to the deeper significance of the movement, a blindness of which only the confirmed intellectualist is capable.

For to the romantic movement there are two very different sides.

The more obvious one is that with which the critics have by this time made us thoroughly familiar. The romantics yearned for union with their twin souls; they were consumed with a nostalgic longing for a largely mythical Greece or an impossible American hinterland; they slipped away from life into an idealized Middle Ages, into the misty and alluring future, or into a theatricalized Catholic Church. From one point of view they were most of them remarkably foolish people, and we can only regard that redecorating and sanitation of their dream castles and ivory towers which is now being undertaken by such critics as Mr Babbitt as a thoroughly wholesome and salutary business.

Yet at the same time it should not escape our attention that the romantic attitude (in a bad sense) does not only represent a pusillanimous evasion of the demands of actuality; it represents also a distorted expression of a search for a very much deeper reality. By nature, we should remember, the romantic belongs to the inspirational, mystically minded, intuitive type. He is able—let us not deny him this—to conceive of a unity, a beauty, a transfiguration of life to which the great run of ordinary mortals remain blind or indifferent. Deep in his heart he cherishes a shining image, intermittently glimpsed it may be, of *what might be,* of a perfection which passes all ordinary human understanding. His strength lies, not in his power of observing actualities, but in his vision of essences. He perceives the potential—and the potential is just as much a reality as that which is actually in manifestation.

But although the romantic is a seer, it is evident that

his seership is of a type which is peculiarly liable to be misinterpreted both by the world and by the man himself. For he has a fatal tendency to make general what is only true of certain places and moments. He idealizes human beings, maintaining in the face of all the evidence that they are perennially what in actuality they are only capable of being for a season. Or, distressed by a sudden sight of them in their more workaday mode, he is seized with a morbid revulsion and denies the reality of the true vision which he was originally vouchsafed. If his imagination is vivid his nerves are weak. He is unable to bear the strain of holding in his mind at the same time a vision of the final union of Dante and Beatrice and a haunting image of the prison, the slaughter-house, and the fever hospital round the corner—although, as the Easterns have always known, it is only by keeping both pictures together in the mind that the lineaments of the Real can be discerned.

So the romantic takes flight. Yet the character of that flight is not without great significance. For it might not unfairly be described as the reflexion of an aspiration towards the true infinite which is cast upon the cloudy, ever-shifting shapes of the false infinite of personal desire. His perversities are revealing, for they indicate by implication the nature of the height from which he has fallen. The image of the mountain on the lake may be inverted, but it none the less points to the substance to which it corresponds. 'No vice is found', says John Scotus, 'but in the shadow of some virtue'.

Admittedly, the romantic is a man who pursues mirages. But a mirage, it should not be forgotten, is an illusory picture of something which is deeply and legitimately desired. And it could, I think, be demonstrated by any talented person with a deep knowledge of true and false mysticism that the ways open to us of apprehending the true infinite could be deduced with remarkable completeness from a study of the characteristic forms assumed by the romantic flight. It is only those who have it somewhere in them to realize the sublime who are really capable of such a degree of emotional extravagance. And, conversely, the unremitting 'soundness' of the classicist is only indicative of his native inability to rise to, or fall from, the plane of true imagination.

But from our present point of view the most important element in the romantic's attitude is his profound sense of the unity underlying the diversity of life. Whether it is a question of thirsting to become one with some being conceived of as perfect, of dying a hero's death for his native land, or of responding to the idea of the brotherhood of man—in each case the basic urge is towards a transcendence of the limits of the personality. It is the heart which calls, the sympathies which are the determining factor. For the classicist, on the contrary, the ideal is no higher than that of *justice*; he envisages a world in which there shall be established a contract of mutual toleration between competing egoisms, a world in which everybody respects the 'rights' of everybody else, but in which everybody, precisely on this very account, is all the more sharply differentiated from his fellows. As Mr Babbitt has written:

> The virtue that sums up all other virtues in the secular order is, as every thinker worthy of the name has always seen, not peace, but justice.

And, as has already appeared, he goes on to say that

> what is needed just now is a revival of the ethical will on the secular level, where it is felt as a will to justice, rather than on the religious level, where it is felt as a will to peace. (*D. and L.* 196-7)

But the romantic demands more. His being is deeply stirred by a sense of the Whole. He is intuitively aware that in so far as we emphasize the separateness of our individualities at the expense of the unity which they together constitute, we cut ourselves off from the deeper levels of being. For the Whole is not merely the sum of the parts of which it is made up, nor even the organ in which they perform a function: it is the only true reality. The individual only becomes truly alive when he is momentarily focussing within his own person the more comprehensive life of the One. Hence his passionate desire to blend his being mystically with that of his fellow-men, his desire, not merely to co-operate and fraternize with them, but, in a sense, to *be* them as well. No Pagan could have said, with Dostoevsky, that 'we are all of us responsible for all of us', or that 'every person participates in the guilt of his fellow-men'. Nor could he have properly understood such a statement as that 'we are all one in Christ'.

Now one of the most bewildering features of this tendency lies in the fact that the manifestation both of naturalistic expansion on the biological plane, and of this genuine sense of mystical communion, bear to the untrained eye a remarkably similar appearance. For it so happens that it is impossible to make any statement relating to this aspect of mystical truth which will not almost infallibly present itself to the legalistic mind as being either a tiresome platitude or an expression of egoism and sentimentality. The determining factor is to be found in a certain quality in the diction which is only to be discerned by those whose consciousness is of the same order as that of the author of the passage. It needs indeed, an exceptional delicacy of imagination to distinguish, on occasion, between the fruits of Rousseauistic phantasy and those of a responsiveness to the true infinite. Yet one represents a pathetic failure in adaptation; the other a vision of the highest possibilities before the race.

And it is just at this point that our dissatisfaction with

Mr Babbitt's treatment of the romantic becomes most acute. For, in spite of his repeated insistence upon the crucial rôle of the imagination, he betrays again and again the most calamitous insensitiveness to this most vital of distinctions. His ideal is control, the ruthless exercise of the *frein vital.* And so concerned is he with this admittedly extremely important element in the moral life that he comes to regard every movement of expansive sympathy, *on whatever level,* with the most undisguised mistrust. He has coined the term 'eleutheromania', designating by it 'the instinct to throw off not simply outer and artificial limitations, but all limitations whatsoever', and he views almost every manifestation of the romantic impulse as an expression of this tendency. To his understanding Rousseau and Keats, Chateaubriand and Wordsworth, Berlioz and Browning, are all more or less on the same plane, for they are all concerned with a process of merging mystically into something beyond themselves—a procedure which the classical humanist can only contemplate with the greatest misgivings.

To examine in detail the manner in which Mr Babbitt's attitude finds expression in his treatment of the finer products of the romantic genius would demand more space than I have here at my disposal. Fortunately, however, any labour expended by me in this direction would be quite gratuitous, for the very good reason that the work has already been performed in a thoroughgoing fashion by a more skilled hand than my own. I will accordingly do no more at this point that direct the interested reader to the concluding chapters of Mr Fausset's penetrating study, chapters in which he will find a convincing demonstration of Mr Babbitt's quite exceptional crudeness in dealing with this aspect of the question.

6. Calculation and Spontaneity

The constitution of man is such that he finds himself related at one and the same time to two different and mutually opposed levels of being: that of the unified and the changeless, which lies above him, and that of the natural and the changing, which lies below him. The task imposed upon him is that of mediating as perfectly as possible between the two—and it is here that the intellectual, critical, consciousness comes into play. For its function lies essentially in reconciling the One with the Many.

Our dissatisfaction with the attitude of the classical humanist lies in the fact that he never achieves such a synthesis with any perfection—although, paradoxically enough, it is precisely with this synthesis that he is theoretically concerned. But in practice he fails, for the reason that he is neither properly orientated to the interior, mystical source of the virtues which he is concerned to display, nor able to give expression to his moral consciousness in terms of actual living. From both possibilities he is cut off by his excessive intellectuality, which at once precludes him from achieving that inward identification with the Good which is enjoyed by the mystic, and renders him incapable of spiritualizing the natural in the manner of the poet. He falls between the Word and the Flesh. He has neither the serenity and joy of the man who is above the law nor the vitality and magnetism of the man who is able to realize the spiritual possibilities of the fleeting occasion.

It is to this that we must now turn our attention. What we have to determine is the success with which the classicist deals with the problem of expression.

We find that his theoretical attitude to the problem seems at first sight to be sound enough. Mr Babbitt writes as follows:

In any particular case there enters an element of vital novelty. The relation of this vital novelty to the ethical or permanent element in life is something that cannot be determined by any process of abstract reasoning or by any rule of thumb; it is a matter of immediate perception. The art of the critic is thus hedged about with peculiar difficulties. (*R. and R.* 355)

And again:

The combining of convention with a due respect for the liberty of the individual involves, it must be admitted, adjustments of the utmost delicacy. . . . But so far as actual conduct is concerned, life resolves itself into a series of particular emergencies, and it is not always easy to bridge the gap between these emergencies or concrete cases and the general principle. . . . A Jesuitical case-book or the equivalent is, after all, a clumsy substitute for the living intuition of the individual in determining the right balance to strike between the abiding principle and the novel emergency. (*D. and L.* 300-1)

In considering the above passages we are brought back once more to the question of the implications of the humanistic position. We have already seen that the classicist can only exercise his specifically 'humanistic' virtues at the cost of what is practically equivalent to transcending the moral plane and developing the consciousness of the mystic. What we now find is that if he is to express his moral consciousness in terms of life he is confronted with the obligation of developing the consciousness of the poet. For just as the mystic excels in realizing the One, so does the poet excel in realizing the Many. And that realization of the Many, that power to spiritualize the transient form, is only acquired when the 'heart' has been quickened. That 'immediate perception' and 'living intuition' of which Mr Babbitt speaks can only be effectively exercised when the emotional, feminine elements in the consciousness have been fully awakened. And it is here particularly that the humanist is so conspicuously ill-equipped. He is only really at his ease when some 'principle' is definitely involved, when some obvious 'ethical purpose' is being achieved. Conversely, the behaviour of those who are living from a deeper centre than that of the detached, critical mind usually presents itself to him as being dangerously unsystematic, extravagant, or inconsequent.

That Mr Babbitt has no real appreciation of what is entailed in the process of living expressively is sufficiently indicated by the passages which we have just considered. For it can hardly escape our attention that his point of departure throughout is not our actual experience of life, but a collection of abstract ethical principles. It is these principles which in his mind come *first,* these principles which the concrete instance can be seen by the moralist to exemplify, these principles which we should be industriously engaged in applying. And where the 'living intuition of the individual' comes into play is not so much in guiding him to respond organically to life as in assisting him in 'determining the right balance' between the universal and the particular. We must all approach the 'particular emergency' with certain standards in our minds and bring them to bear upon the occasion in as judicious a manner as possible. We must temporize here, make concessions there, having all the time a watchful eye upon the 'norm' to which the experience can be referred. The keynote of our behaviour must be *circumspection*—and circumspection entails essentially a condition of pronounced intellectual awareness.

It is evident enough that in treating the question in this rationalistic spirit Mr Babbitt is misrepresenting the whole character of the problem of adapting ourselves to the practical exigencies of life. There are two conditions which have to be satisfied if our human existence is to be rendered tolerable. In the first place life must be established upon a solid moral basis. And in the second place it must as far as possible be spiritualized at every point. The strength of the humanist, and, on a higher level, of the more introverted type of religionist, finds expression in relation to the first of these obligations; the strength of the poet, or the artist, in relation to the second. It is the mark of the true mystic that to a large degree he combines the virtues of the two.

As we have already seen, it is characteristic of the humanist to reinforce his relationship to the Good by formulating and holding before his mind certain ethical 'principles'. And these principles are clearly concerned with the invisible foundations of both individual and social existence. Yet it is evident that foundations have no significance unless some sort of superstructure is erected upon them. And that superstructure is in this case represented by all those activities in life in which there is involved the element of art. It is the final appearance of exuberant beauty and originality which is the ultimate justification of that ethical purpose which is, as it were, all the time being maintained behind the scenes. Morality has, in a sense, a utilitarian significance (even if it is also a good in itself), since it establishes the conditions for that final uniting of the ideal and the sensuous in which life finds its highest expression. The ultimation of goodness is beauty.

Now I do not deny that our concern with intellectual principles may be of the greatest significance. Admittedly, the plane of 'vital novelty' exists at an infinite remove from that realm of general considerations with which the moralist deals; the connexion between the precept that 'charity never faileth' and the action which is demanded of the individual who would apply that precept is tenuous enough. Nevertheless principles do tell. Meditation upon them serves to strengthen our disposition to good: our aspirations find a point of intellectual focus. Further, the crucial moment of spontaneous action may often be led up to by a long period of conscious calculation; the intuition comes into play only when the ground has been prepared by the work of the discursive mind—the mind which lays upon the altar the sacrifice which must ultimately be kindled by the divine spark from above. And we control our experience, again, by formulating as best we can the principles by which our instinctive and intuitive conduct appears in retrospect to have been regulated. We are obliged to systematize our knowledge, if only for the sake of the satisfaction which we derive from contemplating the wider laws of life. Calculation and spontaneity are two mutually complementary principles which come equally into play in the development of consciousness.

But the nearer we draw to this plane of ultimate fulfilment the more do we become dependent upon intuition, instinct, and faith. For without them any real novelty and spontaneity become out of the question; the Word cannot be made flesh. It is only in so far as we become artists that we can effect that union between the One and the Many on which the classicist lays such stress. The individual cannot in this matter regulate his behaviour from his intellectual consciousness alone. He must react with the totality of his being to the challenge of a mysterious and literally incomprehensible reality. In our highest moments our minds are not turned backwards in the direction of the established and the traditional, but prophetically forwards towards that which is to come. We do not live by what *was,* but by what is actually coming into being. We become radiant and unconscious instruments of the spirit, enjoying the bliss which comes from a merging into Something which is infinitely greater than ourselves, and acting more wisely and potently than we are aware. 'No man', says Goethe profoundly, 'knows what he is doing when he acts rightly'. And one might venture to add that, even in the most everyday situations, the only actions which make for charm, surprise, and interior liberation are those which have their source in a momentary rapture. It is only when we have forgotten the past, with its indications of what should and what should not be, that we are a delight to ourselves and others. It is only the timeless instant that is truly living.

It is evident, on the other hand, that in so far as we are living on a less elevated plane than that on which life and art are one, it is upon principles that we chiefly rely. There are long and weary stretches of existence which serve as the preparation for, or appear as the outcome of, those vital moments in which the spirit is able to express itself in a creative fashion. And across those stretches we are carried, unexcitingly but safely, by maxims and rules. We discharge our debts punctually, do our duty, obey the laws of hygiene, respect the conventions of social intercourse. We do not on this account cease to be concerned with realities, though we are concerned with them in a markedly less vital fashion.

But unless we are prepared when the occasion arises to forgo the satisfaction of being intellectually in command of the situation, and to trust in large measure to the intimations of the heart, we are lost. And when it so happens that, through the poverty of a person's being, the moments of creative living present themselves but rarely, or are not responded to when they occur, we meet with that type of life which is exemplary when judged by humanistic standards, but at the same time essentially commonplace and uninteresting. The man or woman is monotonously 'representative' and 'probable'—but nothing much more. Indeed, the most decisive indication of the weakness of a purely humanistic ethic lies just in this fact—that it is possible to conform with considerable faithfulness to the principles of Aristotle and yet remain a dreary and uninspiring figure. For to be delightful, radiant, magnetic, a vehicle of the spirit, it is not enough to be an adept in the art of moderation and sobriety; one must yield oneself with abandon and discrimination to the workings of the creative forces of life.

What that reaction involves it is almost impossible to describe in words. But it certainly has little to do with adapting oneself to 'particular emergencies'. For the romantic and the mystic there are no 'particular emergencies': there is only the infinite and continually diversified manifestation of Reality. And at the time when the individual has become a vehicle for that manifestation he is conscious only of being in an intimate and significant relationship with the world. There is no 'element of vital novelty' entailed, because at that crucial, timeless instant at which he expresses himself (or, rather, something more than himself) there is in his mind no background of normality or probability against which it could possibly present itself as such. It may prove afterwards that he has tempered justice with mercy, qualified courage with prudence, or struck a right balance between magnanimity and severity, but he knows nothing of this at the time. At the moment when the really vital decision is taken he is making a response with his whole being, guided only by a mystical sense of contact with reality. The mind has momentarily become one with the heart; the organism is acting as a unit. The rightness of his behaviour is guaranteed, not by his calculating mind, but *by the inner purity of his being*. He acts with discrimination because, as the result of a type of self-discipline which the classicist finds it almost impossible to understand, he has made himself into a centre through which the higher forces of life can express themselves in a creative fashion.

It is because he fails to understand the nature of this other type of discipline that Mr Babbitt's treatment of the intuition and the imagination is so peculiarly unsatisfying. He makes the serious error of confusing the character of moral action as it appears subsequently after reflection with the character which it presents to the individual at the time. And he thereby misrepresents the truth almost as grossly as did the early Utilitarians when they advanced the preposterous notion that the object of every action was the securing of pleasure.

7. Humanism and Imagination

Our survey is at an end. And it can only lead us to the conclusion that Humanism, regarded as a self-sufficing philosophy of life, can never make any powerful appeal to the great mass of mankind. It is far too 'human' in its attitude to experience! It provides no adequate means for enabling us to pass beyond the frontiers of the self, either inwards into the region of the mystical, or outwards into the region of the poetic. And it consequently offers us no real possibility of emotional liberation.

No philosophy can ultimately win our assent unless it involves an appeal to the imagination, unless in some fashion or other it opens before the mind those strange, haunting, and mysterious perspectives which stir so profoundly the romantic soul. The heart must be satisfied as well as the head. And the heart, when once it has been awakened, responds to the wonder and richness which is inherent in every common situation. The individual acquires a quickened consciousness of the infinite complexity and significance of existence, of the obscure forces and influences which are at work all the time beneath the drab surface of events, of the strange and elusive affinities which exist between the different forms of organic life, of the potencies which lie latent in the soul of man. On a lower level this response takes the form, it is true, of that 'romantic' self-indulgence of which Mr Babbitt so justifiably disapproves. But it represents also a response to the infinite aspect of things which cannot ultimately be denied satisfaction.

The aim of the humanist, however, is that of *localizing the issues*. Apprehensive of liberating the emotions because he has no true centre within himself from which to direct their expression, he would have us dance—or rather proceed sedately along—to a music which has no overtones. His desperate object is to reduce the magical, cosmic, infinite situation to severely 'human' dimensions, to ignore all but the purely 'secular' element in our transactions with one another and the rest of the universe, to limit our interest and activity to those aspects of the question which, because they are clear-cut and readily definable, can be conveniently handled by the legalistic mind. Hence if application is made of certain Christian teachings, they must be 'judiciously employed'—which means that they must be deprived of all but their bare ethical content and thus robbed of any disturbing imaginative appeal; the higher mystical centre from which Jesus worked must be subordinated to that lower rational centre from which the Socratic dialectic is conducted. In the same way that mysterious operation which is entailed in fulfilling one's obligations comes to be thought of exclusively in terms of devotion to 'duty': the limited logical relationship which exists between the individual and the work he is doing is the only element upon which the attention fastens; he acts 'rightly', 'achieves ethical purpose', and that is all. A person's 'virtues', again, are regarded in his capacity to perform certain actions labelled as 'moral', and there the humanist's interest in his behaviour ceases. For he is a rationalist, and the habit of the rationalist is to regard the easily intelligible aspects of every problem as being more real and important than any others.

Directly the heart comes into play, however, we meet

with an exactly opposite tendency, the tendency to insist that *more* is involved in the situation than would appear to the superficial eye. The romantic and the mystic are deeply and rightly persuaded that every human relationship is *momentous,* that it can be seen, when imaginatively realized, to bring the individual into association with the most profound regions of being, that it is, in fact, the point of focus of an infinity of potent, mysterious, and spiritual forces. For 'all is in all, and all in every part'. 'Man', wrote the late Professor Scheler, 'must learn anew the great invisible solidarity of all living beings with each other in the "All-life", of all spirits in the Eternal Spirit'. And Keyserling has expressed the same thought by saying of the individual that 'at every moment of his being he actually reflects a cosmic situation'. So far from the issues being simple and straightforward they are awe-inspiring in their depth and complexity.

But to all these possibilities the humanist remains indifferent. And the result is that his philosophy to a deplorable degree lacks dynamic and inwardness. It is by definition hostile to the notion of the transcendental, to every element in life which cannot be dealt with in intellectual terms. The virtues which it fosters are primarily negative; the humanist is before everything an adept in the art of abstention. He lives within a depressingly restricted horizon; there is never any suggestion that he is conforming to any deeper or more comprehensive purposes than those which are immediately apparent. The 'good' for him is never anything more than what ought to be; he has never deepened his consciousness to the point of realizing that if one does not act rightly one is not merely wrong, but excluded from the realm of reality. Altogether it is a bleak and forbidding outlook, acceptable only to that minority among us who have emancipated themselves from evil without fully entering into the region of the good. And because it allows no place for mysteries, obscurities, and transactions with the Unseen, because it exalts Apollo immoderately above Dionysus, because, as a consequence, it has no poetry, richness, and fire, it will never play any effective part in the regeneration of humanity.

CHAPTER V

SWEETNESS AND LIGHT

OUR concern in this chapter is to determine the potency of culture as a spiritualizing agency—as one of those three spiritualizing agencies in which, as I suggested at the beginning of the book, the humanist places his trust. I propose to deal at considerable length with certain dangers to which, in my opinion, the cultivated among us today are peculiarly exposed. In so doing I shall say a good many things which might be said equally by the more severe type of humanistic philosopher. But I would justify my procedure by the fact that what is here written is addressed primarily to the ordinary educated man and woman, in whose minds the issues in question are by no means clear. My concern is to draw attention to certain points which are *not* being drawn attention to at the present time—even though they are appreciated by the elect.

I am particularly anxious also to make it clear that I am not in what follows doing anything so misguided as to attempt to depreciate the significance of culture. Unless there is culture the meaning of life fails to appear. The only ideal which can possibly satisfy an imaginative mind is one which sets before us the aim of expressing the good, the beautiful, and the true with the greatest conceivable completeness in every department of existence.

All this we can, I hope, take for granted. To be uncultivated is simply to be spiritually impoverished. But although there is palpably an urgent need that the great mass of humanity should be awakened to the significance of this fact, it is no less apparent also that the sophisticated minority need just as seriously to be warned against overvaluing the fruits of cultivation.

1. Civilization versus Salvation

Returning to a distinction which I have already established on an earlier page, the forces which are at work in spiritualizing our lives can be seen to be operative in two clearly defined spheres. In the first place we have those influences which affect the deep moral foundations of every human life, those influences which make for the great basic virtues on the exercise of which the stability of society depends. And in the second place we have those refining influences which can only effectively come into play when these same basic virtues have already found expression. Unless a certain proportion of the population can contrive to be industrious, truthful, temperate, and unselfish in their daily lives, the cultivation of the liberal arts becomes a matter of impossibility. The musician can only display his talent when the piano manufacturers, the electricians, the cleaners, and the management have already done what is required of them. In a word, art comes in when utilitarianism has completed its work.

Ideally, of course, the same principle should apply in the sphere of the individual life. The foundations should come first, the rest being a matter of extending to a wider field that spiritualizing process which has made for a solution of the fundamental problems. First of all the dull, obvious bourgeois virtues and then only afterwards the manifestation of more subtle states of consciousness in terms of speech, dress, architecture, and music.* But

* I ought to make it clear, perhaps, that I am here understanding by 'culture' the expression of the more lofty tendencies in the human soul. From another point of view, of course, it could be maintained that *any* achievement of expression is more desirable than none, and represents, therefore, a cultural advance. 'Not to appear at all in the series

only afterwards—in the moral order, at any rate. That is why the great spiritual teachers have always been so conspicuously silent on the subject of art. They were concerned with the radical issues, with the problem of salvation rather than with that of civilization, and they were well enough aware that when the first is secured 'the rest shall be added unto you'. As the spirit organically unfolds it is impelled to expression in an increasingly wide realm, until ultimately every detail of life, however minute, becomes a means for the manifestation of wisdom and love.

Men and women, however, are so constituted that it is just as easily possible for them to reverse the proper process of progression and begin with secondary considerations first. Æsthetic feeling, intellectual subtlety, delicacy of perception—these are all perfectly compatible with the possession of a radically vicious nature. The fact that Wainwright was a poisoner did not preclude him from having exquisite taste and sensibility. In a word, some people are spiritualized at the core of their beings, others at the periphery. The first condition makes for character, the second for refinement, while both represent an advance upon crass materiality. And although in isolation they are each intolerable, the verdict of experience is that, if we have to choose between extremes, a graceless integrity is preferable to a decorative depravity.

---

of time', the late F. H. Bradley has written, 'not to exhibit one's nature in the field of existence, is to be false and unreal. And to be more true, and to be more real, is, in some way or other, to be more manifest outwardly. For the truer is always the wider'. This would seem to suggest that it is better for a pornographic novel to be well than to be ill written, and for atrocities to be efficiently rather than inefficiently perpetrated. And this may well, indeed, be true. But I must leave this nice question to the philosophers to decide!

This, however, is not all. Through the influence of culture man is induced to purify his perceptions, develop the arts, introduce the element of the spiritual into all those situations in life to the possibilities of which a merely virtuous utilitarianism is indifferent. The individual is not content to express his urge to goodness merely in terms of action; he expresses it also in terms of literature, architecture, and music. A more developed minority rises to the plane of imaginative creation and thereby exerts an uplifting influence upon the rest. For one of the functions of art is moral.

Clearly, if we are æsthetically sensitive we are able to manifest our goodness in a more refined and diversified manner. But to what degree does the practice or the contemplation of art dispose us to righteousness? How far can we look to the æsthetic element in experience to aid us in attaining to salvation, and how far must we regard it simply as an influence which comes into play when it is a question of giving a more comprehensive and sublimated expression to the virtue which we already have within us? It would certainly seem that the more educated today no longer entertain an unduly sentimental conception of its function. Such a statement as that attributed to Mr Ramsay MacDonald to the effect that when a Medici print is found in every workman's home 'the world will have advanced very far on the road of spiritual peace' is likely nowadays to be received with a certain cautiousness, even by his own supporters. Indeed, the more intelligent of them have not failed to take note of the fact that the workers are becoming inspired with a belief in the uplifting power of culture just at the moment when those who are more sophisticated are beginning to conclude that they have exaggerated its moral significance.

Nevertheless, it remains true that culture still offers a dangerous snare to those who have come some way along the path of conscious unfoldment. For in an age like the present, when men have ceased to look upwards to God as the source of their inspiration and power, they are driven almost inevitably into demanding from science, philosophy, and art more than they are legitimately entitled to expect. Particularly do they tend today to be seduced by the appeal of æstheticism. For on the one hand they are aware that life on the plane of mechanization and crude sensationalism can afford no enduring satisfaction to a mature spirit, and on the other they realize that art can open the door for them into a world of beauty and tranquillity. They tend, therefore, to conclude that in culture they are provided with a means for attaining to that state of spiritual equilibrium which men once sought to secure by dedicating themselves to God.

It is this type of attitude which I am concerned with opposing here. My own view is that, to a far greater degree than most educated people are inclined to allow, the possession of culture serves to impede rather than to assist the modern man in coming to grips with the more fundamental elements in his experience.

2. The Epicurean Attitude

Perhaps the most obvious of the temptations to which the more educated are liable to be exposed is that of being beguiled into adopting a hedonistic attitude towards life. To be cultivated is to have become capable of experiencing all manner of pleasant sensations which less mature spirits are precluded from enjoying, and it is not at all surprising that the unwary fall into the trap of seeking these sensations for their own sake. Consider the following passages from Mr J. C. Powys's *The Meaning of Culture* (1930):

> The object of our secret struggle with inertia and futility . . . is simply that we may enjoy the most exciting sensa-

tions that life offers. . . . The whole purpose and end of culture is a thrilling happiness of a particular sort—of the sort, in fact, that is caused by a response to life made by a harmony of the intellect, the imagination, and the senses. . . . That the self which awakens daily to a new plunge into the unknown should be surrounded by a magic circle of memories all orientated towards the same ecstatic sense of life, this alone is real self-culture.

In his brilliant little essay on *Civilization* (1928), Mr Clive Bell describes the delights of refined sensibility in even more seductive terms:

The civilized man is made not born: he is artificial; he is unnatural. Consciously and deliberately he forms himself with a view to possessing and enjoying the best and subtlest. . . . To enjoy life to the full is his end, to enjoy it as a whole and in its subtlest and most recondite details. . . . He chooses his pleasures deliberately. . . . Indeed, it is not denied that the civilized man in search of exquisite pleasure is, and must be, an amateur of exquisite states of mind. . . . The first step towards civilization is the correcting of instinct by reason; the second, the deliberate rejection of immediate satisfactions with a view to obtaining subtler.

It is to be observed that, as conceived by both these writers, the attitude of the 'civilized' man is almost purely *passive* in character. 'Existence secured', says Mr Bell, 'his dealings with life will be mainly receptive'. He is, indeed, a creature who has become an adept in the art of responsiveness, in making the correct, the really sophisticated, reaction to the stimuli to which he is subjected, in being galvanized in a thoroughly superior way. In other words, his attitude to life is that of the sensationalist. And this is to say, again, that he is the victim of an illusion against which the wise have warned mankind ever since civilization began.

The issue is plain enough. Every intelligent person

must necessarily be sympathetic to any form of self-discipline which makes for the refinement of the sensibilities, which awakens people to the more subtle possibilities of life. But he will at the same time be perfectly aware that to seek æsthetic satisfactions for their own sake is simply to court disaster. For there are two kinds of motive which can lead a man to concentrate his attention upon the sensations which are awakened within him by the objects with which he is surrounded, one of them healthy, the other unhealthy. If he examines them primarily with the object of arriving at an understanding of their nature, and of the relations existing between them, all is well; for his concern is not first of all with himself, but with the character of the external Universe. If, however, he discriminates first of all with a view to the securing of pleasure, with a view to identifying those sensations which, if repeated, would prove most agreeable, the result can only be fatal. For the more he concentrates upon the delectable element in his experience the more egocentric and self-absorbed he becomes. The effect of his preoccupation is not that of drawing him out of himself into a wider sphere of being, but that of over-stimulating his exclusive, self-regarding individuality. The objects with which he is presented become degraded from ends to means—means for inducing agreeable states of mind. His feet are set on a road which can only lead in the end to disillusionment and disgust.

The only safe attitude towards æsthetic pleasure is to regard it as something which offers itself by the way, as a delicious, but subordinate, element in the process of orientating oneself to external reality. The primary obligation laid upon us is that of striving at every point to attain to freedom and truth, the manifestation of which is attended by beauty and joy. Once our eyes wander from this central objective we are lost. We become specialists in sensations, and in the end the very pleasures which we are seeking turn to dust and ashes in our mouths.

These are elementary considerations which need not detain us longer here. More important for us to observe is the attitude of the sophisticated towards the satisfactions to be derived from the possession of civilization. Their tendency is to regard them as *superior* to any other. Mr Bell writes, for example:

> Doubtless there are good things in life at which mere force of intellect and character can come; there are better, subtler at all events, which nothing less than manners will buy.

We meet here with a characteristic expression of the 'high-brow' attitude to experience. For the ultra-civilized individual the most precious delights are those which are to be obtained from refined æsthetic perception, from contemplating intricate and subtle relationships, from intercourse with highly sophisticated minds. Before everything, he demands that his sensations should be keen and exquisite. But it is highly disputable whether they are more worth having than certain others which can be enjoyed by the simple.

Is there, for example, anything more fundamentally satisfying than the pleasure which is derived from a wise obedience to the obligations that are laid upon us by Necessity? To live in spiritual and material order, to be fulfilling some relatively humble office in the economy of society, to know that one enjoys the confidence and respect of those with whom one is associated, to pass through life in a condition of calm, fearless equilibrium, to be master of one's passions and desires, to enter imaginatively into the ordinary routine of daily existence so that one derives a deep and sweet peace from undertaking the most simple domestic tasks—are such satisfactions to be regarded as being essentially inferior to those to be obtained from listening with discrimination to Ravel, or from looking at the works of Renoir with a sophisticated eye? Obviously not.

The truth is that only very few people are capable of developing their æsthetic sensibility without paying for the privilege by becoming blind to the more profound, but very much less vivid, delights which it is open to them to derive from their workaday experience. To one degree or another they become sensation-seekers, for whom the most precious moments of life are those in which they are being excited and stimulated by keen, evanescent impressions. It requires a long and painful process of education to make them realize that by cultivating a certain spiritual attitude to life they can come to know a deep and sustaining joy, an interior and abiding peace, that no purely æsthetic experience can afford. But because that peace is the reward of exercising the solid, old-fashioned virtues and not that of keying up the susceptibilities, the cultivated person looks upon it with disdain. It is only when he has pursued the search for refined sensations for a long period that he begins to understand where the more radical satisfactions in life are to be found. As Mr Aldous Huxley has observed, 'the course of every intellectual, if he pursues his journey long and unflinchingly enough, ends in the obvious, from which the non-intellectuals have never stirred'.

3. The Problem of Creativeness

But more fundamental is the point that Mr Bell fails to deal in any satisfactory manner with the central and all-important problem of creativeness. The 'civilized' attitude is essentially responsive, and it is evident enough that we cannot live on responsiveness alone. In order to obtain any adequate satisfaction from life we must not only express ourselves in terms of appreciation, but also in terms of positive outgoing.

As conceived of by Mr Bell 'creativeness' is not an aspect of civilization:

> To be civilized a man must have the taste to choose and appreciate, but—let me say it once again—he need not have the power to create. . . . Creativeness is no more an attribute of the civilized man than of the savage; but discriminating, conscious appreciation is.

But the pleasures which creativeness can afford are, of course, very great: 'It is amongst artists, philosophers, and mystics, with their intense and interminable ecstasies of contemplation and creation, that we must look for our saints'. This is all very well, but it is to be observed that Mr Bell, like a true high-brow, only attaches real importance to that type of creativeness which finds expression in the field of philosophy and the arts, that creativeness, in fact, of which the taste of the 'civilized' person is the complement; once again, the highest pleasures are reserved for the elect.

But, in any case, to be talented is the privilege of a minority. And if we ask how the vast, unendowed mass of men and women are to express themselves in a positive, instead of a merely appreciative, fashion we find that Mr Bell can give us very little help. If I cannot paint pictures, or write poetry, or compose music, if I am incapable of indulging in 'ecstasies of contemplation and creation', how am I to fulfil myself?

It is characteristic of this highly 'civilized' writer that he seeks to evade the issue by creating a false opposition between 'civility' on the one hand and the self-centred and disorderly behaviour of the 'man of action' on the other:

> At its best, the life of action may be an agitated pursuit of what may turn out to be a means to good—good for the actor or more probably for others; but action in itself is worthless, and the state of mind it engenders rarely valuable;

at its commonest, action is a stimulant of bad states of mind in the doer, and to everyone else an unmitigated nuisance.

All that is here said regarding 'action' strikes one as perfectly true. But it is important to point out that there is another type of 'action' which Mr Bell leaves completely out of account: that which has its source, not in vanity and restlessness, but in spiritual obedience. And it is this second kind of action which must of necessity provide the outlet for creative expression in the case of the great mass of mankind.

I shall return to this important question when I come to deal with Mr Middleton Murry's theory of the contemplative life. Meanwhile I will observe only that peace of mind for the ordinary individual lies in his ability to spiritualize his workaday existence, to make it a medium for the expression of truth, love, and power. Then, even if he is unable to achieve creativeness in the sphere of art or philosophy, he will become organically related to the life around him. And although he will be able to enjoy the delights of art only in the passive mode of contemplation, he will come to know others which are even more profound. He will be 'creative' and 'active' in the most vital and satisfying way that is possible for a human being. For he will express in terms of life that which the philosopher can only contemplate and the artist only symbolize. And even if to epicureans like Mr Bell his existence seems distressingly dull and impoverished, he need have no occasion to feel perturbed.

4. Centrifugal and Centripetal

The number of educated people who are so undiscerning as to embrace deliberately a hedonistic philosophy is happily small. The majority have the sense to realize that if they wish to enjoy any fundamental peace of mind they must be prepared to look upon æsthetic pleasure as something which offers itself only by the way. Yet they are still exposed to another danger of a still more insidious nature—that of making their concern with cultural problems a substitute for a more creative type of living.

It is necessary to realize the extent of the temptations with which the educated are today confronted. When once a person has schooled his intelligence and refined his sensibilities to the point of being able to roam freely about that field of civilization on the charms of which Mr Bell has written in such persuasive terms, there is no end to the vistas which open up before his eyes. In the sphere of music and painting every possible type of achievement, ancient and modern, domestic and exotic, is readily accessible to him for study. In that of literature there is a never-ending stream of biography, criticism, and fiction, all incredibly interesting and readable, all artistically produced, all written with a cleverness, a vivacity, a subtle provocativeness, which makes them almost irresistible to any person of imagination and taste. And then there are the fascinating developments in modern science, also presented to one in the most assimilable and attractive form. There is travel if one has the means, and there are the delights of cultivated intercourse. On every hand one meets with the colourful, the complex, the diverting.

Few are able to resist the temptations to self-dissipation which are thus provided for them. They read books, look at pictures, listen to music, very largely for the plain reason that they have been unable to forgo the pleasure of indulging in a certain refined type of sensationalistic gratification. And in this respect they are on exactly the same level as any racegoer or 'movie fan', incidentally creative though their activity may be. They are in search of diversion; they want to be 'interested' and 'intrigued'.

Only, being educated, they demand entertainment of a somewhat subtle type.

Not that such delectation does not play an important part in life. There is no question here of a senseless Puritanical judgment that it is 'wrong'. But the point is that it is for the most part wasteful and unproductive. It represents a failure in spiritual economy and is debilitating in its results. The individual has neglected to impose upon himself a due measure of self-discipline, has permitted himself to be seduced by his senses, has given himself away too lightly. He has not that real hunger which would alone justify his sitting down to the feast.

That only a small number of educated people today should be alive to the perils to which they are exposed in this particular direction is, after all, comprehensible enough. The lack of real culture is so widespread, the need for reputable standards so evident, that it is not surprising that our attention should be primarily concentrated upon overcoming the tendency to revert to barbarism rather than upon seeking for something that is even more fundamental than sophistication. But the fact must be faced that the importance of cultural pursuits is altogether exaggerated. It is uncritically taken for granted by most of us that, provided we address ourselves with due seriousness to a book, a piece of music, or a painting, our behaviour is justified. It is certainly true that we are doing something very much more creative than if we were to spend our time in playing billiards or tearing across the countryside in a car. But it is no less a fact that we may be thereby rejecting certain higher possibilities which are offered to us. It is, indeed, pretty safe to assert that on most of the occasions on which we are thus cultivating our minds we are really allowing ourselves to become related to reality in an unduly easy-going, and therefore uncreative, fashion. It may be better for our souls to read Henry James than Ethel M. Dell, but it does not follow that in submitting ourselves to that refined experience we are not evading our deeper obligations.

It should be sufficiently plain that unless extraversion of this type is balanced by a degree of introversion which is equally extreme, the result can only be devitalization. An equilibrium must be maintained between concentration and diffusion, between the centripetal and the centrifugal tendencies in the soul. The assimilation of objective knowledge must be organic with the development of the inner life. There must be a correspondence between the within and the without. The self must be proportionate to the not-self which it contemplates. Otherwise the individual will be unable to identify himself in any real sense with the external reality which he is studying. He will become overpowered by the form of things, lose himself in a concern with perspectives and correlations. When the mind is active and the deeper sympathies unawakened there can be no other result.

The mark of the genius is that he is able to achieve this balancing of inner and outer to a supreme degree. His interior life is so rich that he can study an enormously wide range of objective phenomena without failing to be adequate to them, without being betrayed into superficiality. There is something within him which can go out and meet that at which he is looking; he carries its complement within himself. But for the average person to aim at such comprehensiveness is merely presumptuous. For he lacks the depth of inner being which alone can justify horizontal expansion on such a scale. Safety will lie for him only in using the discoveries of science and the creations of art as means for confirming and strengthening his own personal apprehensions. Books, poems, and pictures should serve for him as agencies for bringing into the full light of consciousness that which the mind already in some sense possesses, but has not yet properly mastered. They should promote the crystallization into form of impressions and ideas which have their source in deep and personal experience. They should aid in solving a problem, in attaining to a more profound synthesis, in achieving a fuller degree of self-realization. We should look outside ourselves in order to complete a process which has been initiated within.

The fact is that as the inner life of the individual develops he finds himself definitely obliged to restrict the horizontal range of his interests. The objects which he contemplates become too fraught with significance to be attended to and disregarded at will. He hesitates before giving himself to a book or a picture because he knows what it costs him to adapt himself to it. Unless he is quite exceptionally endowed he finds that as his power of response increases the surface movement of his mind becomes diminished. As he becomes more and more alive to the inward aspects of life his thoughts move with less agility and round a smaller number of centres. His culture becomes intensive rather than extensive. The act of attention demands more of him than it used to, and brings with it a greater reward. His interest gradually shifts from the periphery towards the centre. He becomes more concerned with the uniqueness of objects and less exercised regarding the significance which they derive from their place in the horizontal series.

There is, moreover, a further important point to be considered. The person who over-reads, over-listens, over-looks, is not only allowing himself to be drawn too easily away from his deeper centre, but to be drawn away in a definite direction—towards the shallows of experience. For it is evident that, broadly speaking, concern with cultural problems is both an easy and an agreeable pursuit, and one which makes far less exacting demands on the individual than do those which are involved in growth in the dimension of the vertical.

Why? For the simple reason that he is dealing with life at a remove. The foundation for his studies is provided by the immediate response of certain more vital people to experience. At some point or other men and women have exposed themselves barely to reality, have ventured abroad, have exercised their wills in the face of opposition, have passed through the fires of spiritual purgation. Their actual deeds, or the art forms which they have created, then become material for cultured interest. That which was born out of a direct act of adaptation to life is analyzed, classified, evaluated, savoured, placed in its proper perspective. Action is translated into consciousness.

It is to be observed, further, that even this degree of intimacy with reality is only achieved by a minority. Thought in this field centres to an overwhelming degree, not merely on facts abstracted from life itself, but on ideas for which they have provided the inspiration. The mind of the student is working upon something essentially artificial, something which has already been shaped by the human intellect before it is presented to his attention. His subject-matter consists of documents (and only rarely original documents at that), ideas, schemes of classification, critical observations upon critical observations. His intelligence is like a factory which handles only 'semi-products'; the material has already passed through a preliminary process of treatment before it reaches his hands.

Further, he deals with the situation on his own terms. He selects from the mass of human experience certain elements which in life appear, not in artificial isolation, but associated with others which he would probably find distasteful and disconcerting to encounter. He picks out what he pleases and considers it at his leisure. The facts which he contemplates have been accumulated under conditions which he himself is not called upon to face. He watches the history of individuals and peoples from across the frontiers of space and time, without being called upon to accept their implications. His concern is with anthologies, distillations, with the gold which remains when the painful process of refining has been completed. Particularly is he shielded from the more disturbing types of human association. He learns from books what it feels like to go round the Horn before the mast, to dwell in a slum, to live the life of a secret service agent. The fiery, disruptive influence which is radiated from a powerful personality reaches him only through the insulating medium of letterpress. Modern technical developments have rendered it possible for him to contemplate the spectacle of men storming, praying, cursing, and rhapsodizing from a perfectly safe distance. He can bring the interview to a conclusion whenever he feels disposed to do so by replacing the volume on the shelf, closing the portfolio, switching off the wireless or the gramophone. With a minimum of labour or embarrassment he can skim off the richest cream of human experience.

5. Primary and Secondary

It remains to consider the effect of all this upon the psychology of the individual.

The first point to observe is that, as the result of his excessive concern with the form of things, with life in its horizontal aspects, his thought comes to play all the time round objects which exist at a remove from reality, objects which have been created by a subtle process of simplification. His attention becomes steadily shifted from the plane of life to the plane of ideas. His mind becomes unduly sensitized to abstractions and correspondingly unreceptive to the significant and unanalyzable immediacies. Theories become more real for him than the experience which originally served them for a foundation. The characteristic point of departure for his thought is not that direct and disturbing experience of life which fascinates the mind of the artist, but something which is brought into being by leaving out of account all the facts which most profoundly disturb and perplex.

It is not that such people are not conscientious and painstaking as thinkers. The point is that their data are wrong. They may be rigorous enough in working out the implications of their assumptions, but at the basis of the whole edifice is an initial shrinking from facing the really challenging facts. They are like inferior artists who, in spite of their talent and application, fail to achieve anything significant because they are all the time accepting without protest certain conventional values which are repudiated by those of a more sincere type. Typical of their attitude is that of the academic moral philosopher whose mind moves serenely enough in the realm of abstract considerations, but who directly he proceeds to illustrate his conclusions by examples reveals himself as being almost crudely insensitive to the more delicate spiritual issues in life.

But apart from the tendency towards superficiality which is fostered by the very nature of this intellectualistic approach to experience, there comes into play also the important element of morality. Such a concentration on critical appreciation is continually threatening to bring about a disastrous divorce between consciousness and action.

Take first the question of introspection. It is clear that in order to understand the fruits of spiritual experience one must first be aware from within of what that experience means. This, however, only up to a point. And it is just in this fact that the danger for the more educated lies. For it so happens that without really facing the deeper problems of life one can yet acquire a sufficient acquaintance with the fundamental issues to be able to enjoy their presentation in terms of art, while at the same time having no strong impulse to modify the actual conduct of one's own life. Hence we find among the cultivated numbers of people who are sufficiently sensitive to read Proust or Ibsen with pleasure, but whose passion for truth never quite reaches the point of provoking them to act. Their responsiveness thus serves only to provide them with the opportunity of indulging in a sort of spiritual parasitism: they are thereby enabled to deal with the deeper problems of existence in purely symbolic terms. The consequence is that on the one hand they never come to understand the creations of the artist in any real sense, and on the other their inner lives are poisoned by the lack of continuity between their consciousness and their being.

No truth can be properly understood until it is not merely contemplated, but actually lived out. And here the contrast between the artist who has created the work and the cultivated person who is admiring it presents itself in the sharpest relief. For that which is written, composed, or painted by a true artist represents only, as it were, one facet of his personality. The same consciousness which finds expression in creation on the plane of the imagination finds expression also on the plane of life. He may, indeed, be unbalanced, infantile, or morbidly sensitive; the man of inspiration only rarely succeeds in attaining to a true equilibrium. But his deepest striving, at least, is to live organically, to translate realization into action. The peculiarly realistic attitude to experience which finds a reflection in his art is reflected also in his dress, his speech, his way of living, his attitude to human relationships. All these branches spring from the same root.

The case of the average cultivated person is widely different. He is lavish enough in his appreciation, but he shrinks perceptibly from involving more than his mind in his association with truth and beauty. He reads, and professes to enjoy, such writers as Katherine Mansfield and D. H. Lawrence. Yet in almost every paragraph over which his eye passes there is either a direct or an implicit challenge to his actual mode of living. If he were really to identify himself fully with the standards of truth and sincerity which are maintained in the works which he is studying he would almost inevitably be driven to change his whole mode of existence. These people refuse to make compromises; he himself is compromising all the time. They stand for spiritual freedom; he is the slave of a hundred conventions. They are prepared at every point to take risks; he is disturbed by any prospect of uncertainty or unpleasantness. They are almost cruelly sincere in their personal relations; he is afraid of either speaking or hearing the more intimate truths. It is difficult, therefore, to regard him as being anything else but a sentimentalist—a sentimentalist who is violating his integrity by attempting to live on two different planes of reality at the same time.

Piquantly enough, there are no people who are more sensitive to this fact than the very artists whose work gives rise to this particular state of affairs. Towards the poor and simple they are habitually more than kindly. Up to a point they are even able to tolerate the vulgarian, provided only he has a certain degree of vitality. But for the refined people who are content to come to terms with truth on the plane of the imagination only, they have a barely concealed contempt. In one sense, indeed, art is the real enemy of culture.

Finally, we have to consider the fact that the most serious price paid for this failure to take action is that the individual never really gets down to those issues which are important, not in the abstract, but for him alone. In simple terms, he never properly finds himself. He may have lofty ideals, he may be tolerant, chivalrous, sweet-natured; but while he is still living on this plane of generalities he never fully possesses the truths which he contemplates. The whole man has never become completely involved in the process of adaptation. The steel needs still to be tempered. As a result, he can never bring the full weight of a matured personality to bear upon the issues with which he is dealing. It is for this reason that the speaking and writing of the more academic type of thinker usually have about them that faint and unconvincing quality which is so familiar, yet which it is so difficult to define with any exactitude. What is said is true; it may even be profound. But somehow it has no cogency, sting, or power of penetration; it does not come from the right place. It is not the fruit of real personal experience, not truly possessed. We nod our approval, yet a short time after we have laid down the book we find it extraordinarily difficult to recall what it is we have read. The light has not been radiated from a true centre, but reflected glamorously from the clouds. We turn with relief to the living writer, even if he is treating of less significant themes.

What it all comes to is that the average cultivated person is spiritualized at the periphery but not at the core. Everything is all right but the foundations. There is sensitiveness, imagination, logicality, urbanity, but no true serenity, and little poise or power. The man at once charms us with his command of the more superficial levels of experience and disappoints us by his failure to deal with fundamentals. His consciousness is not irrigated from the central fount of his being; the sap has not mounted from the roots. Deep down he is the whole time on the defensive. Although he moves freely and confidently about on the plane of ideas he is defenceless against one ray from the solar plexus. Silence discovers him. When he is deprived of his polished intellectual weapons he finds himself unable to compel or persuade. In spite of all his sophistication he is distressed by the sense of a dreadful void within. Although he knows a great deal, what he *is* is something relatively insignificant.

Unfortunately, however, it may take him a long time to realize these things with any completeness. For the very wealth of his superficial knowledge and attainments serves to blind him to the fact that at bottom he is divided against himself. The words of Jesus regarding the rich man's difficulty have here a significant enough application. For between the more highly educated person and the truths which he so urgently needs to know there hangs the richly embroidered curtain of his own sophistication. He has become too sensitive to complexities to be able to perceive the simple. When an unlettered artisan has gone astray in respect to his more radical relationships with life, there is little between himself and reality to disguise from him the truth. But when a man can appreciate Stravinski, find his way about modern philosophy, and talk with discrimination about Picasso and Jung, the situation is entirely changed. There are so many graces and faculties at his command, so many ways in which he can satisfy indirectly his desire for the good and the beautiful, that it is infinitely more difficult for him to realize the fact that at bottom he is restless, dissatisfied, and uncertain of himself.

Yet it would seem that the more discerning among us are now beginning to realize in some degree how limited and insecure their control over experience really is. They have no desire to depreciate the importance of cultural attainments; that would be mere foolishness. But they perceive that such attainments tend only too readily to deflect the attention from those more radical issues which we are bound to face if we wish to be at peace with ourselves and the world. There must surely be something missing if at the same time people know so much, are so exceptionally sensitive, and are yet so deeply unhappy. Is it possible that we cannot get along after all without that compensating inwardness which is the fruit of adopting a more mystical attitude to life?

Nor does this consciousness fail to find a certain reflection in the attitude of the masses towards the educated classes. They are beginning to be beset with an obscure feeling that our intelligentsia are behaving in an excessively self-indulgent manner. Our professors, our writers, our critics, all enjoy remarkable privileges. They are free to study and reflect at their leisure, and this for the most part in agreeable material circumstances. And this entails responsibility. The debt must be paid back, Society indemnified for placing them in such a favourable situation. Yet when their less fortunate fellow-men turn to them for light they are usually met with disappointment. On the more external features of life they can discourse with freedom, authority, and charm. But regarding the deeper issues they are in a degree of confusion which strikes one as disproportionate to the facilities at their disposal for elucidating truth.

Yet in these days when we can no longer confidently look to ecclesiastical authority for light, who will aid us if not they? Mr Everyman is beginning to feel that these people lack the knowledge they should possess, for the plain reason that they are not prepared to pay the price for obtaining it. If he wants illumination he finds himself listening instead to the tortured artists or the ascetic followers of the mystic path. The others, he feels, are too comfortable to discover the really significant facts. 'I perceive now,' says a character in one of Mr Aldous Huxley's novels, 'that the real charm of the intellectual life—the life devoted to erudition, to scientific research, to philosophy, to æsthetics, to criticism—is its easiness.

It's the substitution of simple intellectual schemata for the complexities of reality; of still and formal death for the bewildering movements of life'. The comment is as acute as it is outspoken. And one cannot but feel that it is thoroughly justified.

6. The Gateway to Reality

If we enquire by what means the attention of the inordinately intellectualistic thinker is to be deflected from ideas to essentials, we find ourselves inevitably returning to the conception of the unified consciousness. The important, the *revealing*, facts only disclose themselves to the man or woman who has been spiritually quickened, and whose heart and head have as a result become properly co-ordinated. The consequence is an awakening to the significance of all manner of aspects of experience which the theoretically minded habitually either ignore or treat in an excessively perfunctory manner. Both the poet and the mystic are deeply aware that the really important principles, the principles that one needs to understand if one wishes to become whole, are discovered only as the result of attending to a type of fact which simply does not catch the eye of the person whose deeper emotional nature has not been stirred.

But the conditions for becoming aware of such facts are severe enough. In the first place the individual must be prepared not merely to associate himself with the simple and humble, but to enter with great completeness into the conditions in which he will then find himself. Then, provided that he surrenders himself with patience and humility to this new type of experience, a new light will slowly break in upon his soul. The swift and easy movements of his mind will be arrested; he will repeatedly find himself *stopped*, brought to a halt by obscure yet significant situations which he cannot master with his facile, logical intellect. In other words, his instincts and intuitions will at last begin to become active. He will orientate himself to reality, not with his critical intelligence alone, but by becoming obedient to a deeper centre in his being, a centre which only becomes operative when something more feminine in his nature has been aroused. The determining element in his behaviour will now be his sense of the mysterious flow of life between himself and his fellow-men. On the one hand that flow may, to his surprise, be broken by actions which appear to his self-conscious mind as being eminently reasonable and judicial; on the other it may be fostered by conduct which he would normally be disposed to regard as irrational or inconsequent. But this fact he is obliged to accept. Indeed, in course of time he is only too willing to submit to these bewildering conditions for the sake of the deepened sense of reality which comes from obeying the more creative impulses in his being.

Not that he does not eventually come to perceive that his apparently inconsequent actions are really governed by definite principles. But they are not the sort of principles with which he is at home. They pertain to what I have earlier referred to as the Science of Being; they serve to throw light on the problem of attaining to a deeper spiritual integrity, of relating oneself in a vital fashion to one's surroundings. And their distinctive feature lies in the fact that the data on which they are based are derived to a very large degree from those intimate personal contacts which the intellectual are so unwilling to face.

But this process of re-education is, I must repeat, extremely painful in character. The poet is not born without great travail. It takes a long time for the average over-intellectualized person to realize that in this particular sphere of reality he must be prepared to receive illumination from the most unsuspected quarters, to learn his lessons in completely unfamiliar terms, to strain his ear to catch overtones to which he previously paid little attention, to abandon some of his most cherished preconceptions, to bare himself to truths which he has not hitherto been prepared to face. Yet only at this price can spiritual be substituted for merely intellectual knowledge.

The truth is that most people who have received a good education tend to exaggerate the importance of the part which it plays in giving insight into the deeper values of life. True, if an individual already possesses insight, then an intellectual training will certainly help him to make use of it. And the ability enjoyed by the educated person to identify and compare different types of psychological experience may assist him in understanding his own reactions. But it remains true that the fundamental elements in the spiritual life can be apprehended and interpreted quite effectively by people who have very little acquaintance with the categories of sophisticated thought. In these matters it is the heart which discerns. If the knowledge revealed to the heart can be brought into relation with that other knowledge which is manipulated by the head, so much more richness to the personality. But even when the head is a negligible element in the partnership the person can be a powerful force for the regeneration of society.

The point is that the particular kind of awareness which the educated derive from dealing with experience in its more intellectual aspects hardly comes into play at all when it is a question of the deeper laws of life. The attention then becomes concentrated upon a certain type of datum which the unsophisticated person can identify and handle just as effectively as can any other—often more effectively, indeed, than the person who is highly educated. We find ourselves in a region in which the vital issues are brought into focus by such factors as acts of devotion, simplicity of behaviour, humbleness of spirit.

The ability of the member of the intelligentsia to indulge in fine operations of analysis, to create elaborate schemes of classification, to discriminate between subtle types of æsthetic impression, here confers very little advantage upon him. His refined perceptions will, it is true, prove of the greatest value to him at a later stage in his development in this direction, but at the beginning of the path it would probably be nearer the truth to describe them as an impediment to progress.

We may draw from this an important conclusion. If anything in the nature of a religious revival ever takes place in this country—and there are those among us who believe that the trend of events is in that direction—we shall be prudent not to expect the educated classes to play any more important a part in it than that which is played by people of quite humble origin and pretensions. Spiritual power, insight, and authority—these things are apt at such an epoch to manifest themselves in the most unexpected places, to the confusion of the orthodox. A tram-driver who has been spiritually quickened in the way in which certain slaves were once quickened at the beginning of the Christian era, or as certain Quakers were quickened in the seventeenth century, is a figure to be reckoned with—particularly in a society which, like our own, is beginning to regard the capacities of its intelligentsia with distrust.

7. Artist and Priest

The facts that are important, then, are those which most typically arrest the attention of the artist. But this is not to say that we can safely turn to him for guidance in our most serious psychological difficulties. For although he is usually remarkably realistic in his attitude to experience, it is only rarely that he possesses any really profound spiritual insight. Indeed, the very purity of his artistic vision makes it particularly difficult for him to understand many of the deeper issues with which man finds himself confronted. In view of the growing tendency today to regard such writers as D. H. Lawrence as the latter-day successors of a discredited priesthood, it will not, perhaps, be out of place to enquire at this point into the real extent of our debt to the artist in relation to the problem of self-fulfilment.

He is distinguished above all by his passionate sympathy with everything which leads to a greater measure of life. But by ' life ' he understands for the most part that which is untrammelled, spontaneous, individualized, and rich in quality. So long as the lover is ardent, the dancer fleet, the warrior courageous, the fact is enough for him. His eye is for character and proportion. He can tolerate squalor, provided only it be typical. If any act of destruction has about it an epic quality it is thereby condoned in his eyes. All that he asks of the individual is that he shall boldly be himself—whatever sort of self he may possess. He has no revulsion from anger or lust, provided only that they be pure. His first concern always is that the manifestation shall have form. Better a spirited and sincere outpouring of rage than characterless monotony. He can even derive satisfaction from the negation of life if only that negation becomes through its perfection an expression of life in another mode. Hence, although he shrinks from the ascetic, it nevertheless has for him deep artistic significance. The devitalized is only the vital in an inverted form. The bones of the skeleton can fascinate as much as the bloom on the cheek. He is pre-eminently sensitive to the pattern, the spectacle, the architecture of the scene. He is more beguiled by the contour than by that which it circumscribes. He is not interested in substance, but in structure, rhythm, pulsation. What disappoints and distresses him more than anything is the featureless, the smudgy, the corrupted, the product of compromise or fear.

The artist *qua* artist is almost completely indifferent to considerations of morality—except in so far as there lies, perhaps, a certain immorality in failing to achieve distinctness and individualization. And although as a human being he is acutely sensitive to the difference between good and evil, joy and pain, it is inevitable that his heightened consciousness of the æsthetic aspects of life should affect his attitude to ethical problems. The man for whom such things as sexual passion, anger, extravagance, and destruction have a pronounced spectacular value cannot in the nature of things judge them with the detached serenity of the saint. He cannot help deriving a deep satisfaction from any rich expression of life, and this satisfaction is bound to have a subtle influence upon his moral judgments. The exhibition of vitality of any type tends to become for him its own justification, to be redeemed if only it be invested with character. His standpoint is that of the Greeks who on a famous occasion pardoned a convicted criminal on the score of her superb physical beauty. This is not true of such an artist as Chekhov, but it is true of a good many thinkers whose moral judgments are palpably coloured by their exceptional sensitiveness to the æsthetic—as we shall see when in the following chapter we come to deal with the theories of Mr Middleton Murry.

More important, however, is the fact that the artist's conception of what constitutes vitality and creativeness is usually conditioned to a dangerous degree by his extreme sensitiveness to the physical, the biological, aspects of experience. His standards are essentially those of the human all-too-human being. He asks of people nothing more than that they shall live up, not so much to their ideal, as to their more characteristic selves. A periodical yielding to anger, brutal physical desire, or extravagance, he regards as being simply incidental to being a full-blooded man or woman. All that he demands is that passion shall be sincere and unalloyed. He is, indeed, deeply suspicious of all idealism: it offers a threat to the preservation of roundedness and completion. The man who is too concerned with controlling himself is in danger of losing his spontaneity—an unforgivable crime. In a word, his attitude is markedly naturalistic. I sulk, I weep, I rage, I become quarrelsome, I take myself off abruptly, I recklessly squander my (and possibly your) savings, because I have a deep, and oh! so pure, impulse to do so. If I failed to obey such promptings I should violate myself. At all costs the unimpeded flow of life!

Needless to say, this romantic, feminine, expansive attitude is sharply opposed both to that of the classical humanist and to that of the religious thinker. And if we enquire where exactly the point at issue between them lies we find that the decisive factor is the element of time. The mark of the more passionate type of artist is that he is ever eager to achieve a synthesis which bears its fruit here and now. He is beautifully sensitive regarding everything which makes for vitality and harmony, but that vitality and harmony must be manifested without too much delay, must be there, living and vibrant before his eyes. I am not referring to the improvident bohemian who is concerned only that the party shall be a success, even though he is left penniless at the end of it. I am thinking, rather, of the attitude of the typical artist towards those modes of self-fulfilment which entail the frustration of the life-impulse on the biological plane. For although he is accomplished enough in the art of ordering and harmonizing, this is only within the limits of a relatively restricted scheme. He has a keen eye for the appropriate and the teleological. He perceives with divine intuition what should be the characteristic occupation of this person, who is the proper mate for this other, how the elements of labour and relaxation, of concentration and diffusion, should be balanced in a properly conducted existence. He knows precisely when and how to dance, mourn, make love, contemplate, congregate, seclude oneself. He gets the proportions exactly right. But they are the proportions in a unity which is, as it were, too narrowly complete in itself. Any failure to achieve or maintain it he is disposed to regard as being so much wastage, as a dead loss, as forming an empty and ugly gap. And here, again, I do not mean that the enlightened artist does not attach a positive significance to the more painful elements in our experience. But his tendency is to fasten upon their æsthetic significance, to regard them as providing him with sensations which, even if they are distressing, yet serve to heighten his vitality. Mr Powys's satisfaction in hating and defying the malignant Being who in his view is responsible for the evil in the world is typical of this point of view. Misery and deprivation are welcomed because they are considered as having their place in the texture of human experience, because without them the picture would not be complete. The basis of the attitude is a courageous desire to accept life in its totality. But the acceptance is essentially blind.

The mark of the more mystical thinker, on the contrary, is that he is intuitively conscious of the wider cycle in which our lives have their place. He is concerned with making a more fundamental type of synthesis than that which is entailed in that harmonizing of the superficial elements in experience which for the artist means so much. The order in which he participates is of a more comprehensive type. In Mr Murry's terms, he is aware of the significance, not only of biological, but also of metabiological, unity. And this means that he attaches to such factors as atonement, asceticism, self-abnegation, expiation, renunciation, an importance which the typical artist can scarcely comprehend. He is aware that by accepting limitation in the proper spirit he can attain to a freedom that is infinitely more satisfying than that which is realized by the man who is living 'spontaneously'.

As a result, there are many kinds of spiritual difficulties in which the artist can offer us little help. He may, indeed, have an extraordinary capacity for perceiving the respects in which the individual fails to realize his inner freedom. When it is a question of liberating the self from its interior, psychological bonds, the assistance which he can offer us is simply invaluable. Be yourself! Admit that there are all manner of passionate, savage, and tender feelings within you! Follow your intuitions and instincts boldly! Cast away fear and radiate joyfully the light within your soul! All this is admirable. But it is no less apparent that he has no counsel to offer us regarding the equally momentous problem of submitting ourselves to external necessity. His attitude towards its workings, in fact, is usually almost infantile—one of impatience, petulance, or puzzled despair. Or, as I say, he merely transfers the experience to the sensationalistic plane.

The truth is that he is an imperfect realist. He can deal with life properly only in its positive phase of outgoing, manifestation, expression. The fabric of his philosophy is all warp and no woof. Directly the element of limitation comes into play he either repines or rebels. Yet it is plain that if we look at life realistically we are obliged to recognize that the problems raised for us by the great fact of Necessity are no less urgent and complicated than any other with which we are confronted. The technique of dealing with this phase of life is just as intricate as that called for in achieving expressiveness. And it is a technique which is understood completely only by the saint. Where the artist teaches us the art of forthgoing, the saint teaches us above all the art of submitting. Both must be mastered by any spirit that wishes to lay claim to maturity. But the principles of the second are only to be understood by the individual who has died to his natural self and been reborn in the Eternal.

8. Historical and Unhistorical

One of the chief reasons for the modern intellectual's disposition to depreciate the significance of the instinctive and intuitive elements in our consciousness is to be found in the type of education which he has received. That Science of Being which we so urgently need to cultivate has at present no place in the curriculum of the modern university. There is liberal provision made for the study of the objective side of existence, but concern with the more interior aspects of life is represented only by the discipline of Moral Philosophy (which has, of course, scarcely any bearing upon actual problems of conduct), purely descriptive Psychology, and, for a minority, something called Pastoral Theology. The result is that the fundamental issues remain essentially untouched.

Distinctive of the body of teaching which is imparted to the students in our universities is the fact that it can be assimilated, organized, and formulated without any really serious demands being made upon their powers of introspection. They are never required, in order to verify or identify their conclusions, to look really deeply within. Or let us say, rather, that they are never required to undertake any exploration which is likely to involve them in spiritual uneasiness or distress. If they do, the result is only that they bewilder their examiners. They are normally occupied in handling data which have been created by abstracting from the individual situation certain relatively simple features which lend themselves to forming a point of departure for abstract theorizing. And the result is that the values which they acquire by this process are not the values which really tell, not the values which provide them with any real command over their experience.

What they contrive to do instead is to achieve a sham maturity of a peculiarly irritating sort. It would seem, on the surface, that the product of this system has attained to a state of poise and serenity after having reviewed life judicially in all its manifold aspects. What has actually happened is that he has received an intensive training in circumspection. He has acquired, in an extreme degree, what Nietzsche once described as the 'historical' attitude of mind. That attitude is distinguished by the fact that the observer is always standing in the midst of a no-man's land of thought. He is not looking at the subject from any one point of view: he is situated at the centre where they all meet. The result is that his truth is nobody's truth, his landscape one which has no lights and shadows because it is illuminated from all directions at once. He can make no vital affirmation, because he is only concerned with the colourless residue which remains when all the vital affirmations have cancelled one another out. Acutely aware that every attitude of mind must of necessity have its complement somewhere, he is careful not to go too far in any one direction for fear of thereby doing an injustice to an opposing tendency. Hence a sterile and monotonous 'soundness' which has a deceptive resemblance to that equilibrium which is the result of having achieved a truly vital synthesis. For although he is infinitely tolerant, conscientious, and critical, it may yet truthfully be said that he *knows* nothing: he is aware only of that which comes into existence when different external aspects of truth are confronted. And this is not—not for such as him at least—a further truth, but a lifeless abstraction. Even after leaving the institution with high honours he remains a babe at heart who has yet to learn his first lessons about life by experience in a wider world.

Not that this particular type of awareness is not of considerable importance in its proper place. In all sorts of departments of life we cannot get along without critical surveys, the nice balancing of claims, the bird's-eye view. And we ought to be duly grateful that our universities continue to turn out men and women who are so admirably qualified for this type of work. All I want to suggest is that this *extensive* aspect of knowledge is fostered by modern higher education to an undue degree at the expense of that *intensive* aspect by which it should properly be complemented. I do not refer to specialization in a given field of study, but to something deeper. The best way I can bring out the issue, perhaps, is by saying that young people should be taught to face, and to answer, such questions as: What am I essentially? What does this subject really mean to *me*? What do I really feel when this particular chord is struck? In a word, to employ again the terminology of Nietzsche, they must learn to become 'unhistorical' and thus to achieve a true spontaneity.

Why are most men and women who have passed through a university so painfully *unreal*? Surely because they are almost incapable of making any personal statement, or of taking any action which is really individual. They are essentially circumspect—and circumspection in the wrong connexion makes for the death of the spirit. They have been taught by their mentors to be hospitable to every attitude and theory, to do them all justice, to take all possible factors into account. The result is that their capacity for inspiration and initiative has severely suffered. They are equally conscious of every possibility, and the result is that all possibilities are equally closed to them.

The root of the whole trouble is an exaggerated estimate of the value of a liberal education. It is assumed without justification that the more things you know the greater your command over experience. And this is surely not true. Certainly a man should have a proper knowledge of those subjects which he needs to master in order to fulfil himself. But the number of those subjects is far smaller than the ordinary 'educated' person is prepared to believe. The fact should be faced that the man who is truly vital cannot but be absolutely *indifferent* to a vast range of information. He may want it some time, but he does not want it *now*. If he is living up to his highest possibilities he will simply refuse to assimilate it. In relation to the mass of men—even of exceptional men—it remains true that to be properly alive is to be preoccupied. The individual does not even want to hear about certain things. He refuses to admit even that he *ought* to hear about them. If his creative outlet does not lie in that particular direction he presents to those enlightened liberals who want him to 'take an interest in' the Polish Corridor, the Socialist Movement, the newest discoveries about vitamines, germ cells, or electrons, a wall of impenetrable passivity.

The genius, of course, stands apart; but we are not discussing genius. And clearly there are certain people also whose function lies precisely in undertaking surveys and compilations. The man who is born to exercise this particular function will be aware of the fact and rejoice in his work. And one perceives also that the 'unhistorical' person can, if necessary, become absorbed in almost anything, however remote it is from his own preoccupation, provided only that he finds himself related to it in an organic fashion. But he will be adamantine in his refusal to be seduced by 'interesting' ideas, in his determination to resist the contagion of other people's enthusiasm. He has a standing-place of his own, and from it he refuses to shift. And because he has taken root he ultimately bears fruit.

Is it not apparent that what is really needed if people are again to become vital and fulfilled is not an extension of education, but its restriction? That we must learn to live more vertically and less horizontally? At present we are confronted with the spectacle of a race of beings who are everywhere at once and at no one place in particular. There is universality, but no point of focus. There is an abundance of tolerance, but no passionate predilection to make that tolerance significant. The whole is never seen, for the reason that all the parts are perceived simultaneously. Further, the individual, as a result, is hardly ever able to behave with real deliberation. He is not acting because he knows deep within his being that this is what he must do at this particular juncture. He is not acting because he has discovered by resolute introspection that he will violate himself if he behaves otherwise. He has not identified himself with his deeds in any profound sense. He acts usually because, after balancing things up, this or that seems to be what is left, what appears, after all, to be the best thing to do.

But it is almost certainly *not* the best thing to do. In such matters the critical intellect cannot decide; the decision must be made with the whole of the man's being. Otherwise it is only a pseudo-decision, the result of having looked *outwards* upon the concrete possibilities before one, but not *inwards,* so as to discover the direction in which the deeper life is flowing within the soul.

It should be added that this process of self-limitation does not, as might easily be imagined, restrict the sympathies. On the contrary, it is a notable fact that the man who has truly found himself is peculiarly sensitive to the individuality of others. Through attaining to real self-hood (which is submission to a greater Self) he becomes more alive than he was before to the self-hood of others. He respects their being more, because he has succeeded in becoming something definite himself. He is tolerant of opinions because he knows from within what is entailed in the sincere affirmation of belief. And, finally, he exercises a salutary influence upon the unindividualized, abstract, universalistic people who are so typical of our present age, for by his very presence he impels them to look within and set about being something particular themselves.

9. The Two Unities

But here, again, we must not permit ourselves to be led astray by the artist. One of the effects of our inordinately 'cerebral' condition is a deep hunger for the immediate and spontaneous life of instinct. The highly intelligent, but painfully thin-blooded, individual cannot fail to realize that the man who is living from his solar plexus is alive in a far more intense and satisfying fashion than he is himself. So he reads with avidity the pages of such writers as D. H. Lawrence and Mr J. C. Powys and even makes desperate efforts to achieve the same dynamic spontaneity himself.

Almost invariably, however, he fails—and the reasons for this failure are extremely interesting. It is to the immense credit of such writers as Lawrence that they have realized that the present calculating, ultra-selfconscious, sceptical generation is cut off from the deeper roots of its being. The self is unhappily and fatally divided, the mind and instincts at war, the will consequently paralyzed. Such a state of affairs—analyzed with masterly skill by Mr Fausset in his *Proving of Psyche*—is too agonizing to be endured; we must obtain at all costs some type of relief.

And here two paths open before us. On the one hand we can, after a severe struggle, attain to a condition which lies *beyond* that of the divided self—and this is regeneration, the unification of the consciousness, what Mr Murry describes as the birth of the New Man. In this fashion we return on a higher level to that union with Nature which the primitive, unawakened man enjoys only on the plane of the unconscious.

On the other hand, we may seek to revert, to relapse into that condition of pre-conscious spontaneity which leads up to the discovery of self. This is only a pseudo-solution to the problem. But it is a solution which is being attempted with great frequency by the consciousness-ridden, devitalized man of today. He tries in one way or the other to 'go native', to worship at the shrine of Lawrence's 'dark gods', to respond to the deep, stirring rhythm of elemental life. But the attempt is abortive. Such success as he enjoys is intermittent, and paid for by a supervening enervation. For he is failing to be true to his birthright as a civilized Western European man. We cannot now go back and 'live below the diaphragm'. We must, as Mr Adrian Stokes has so forcibly shown in his *Sunrise in the West*, achieve that higher spontaneity which is the final culmination of calculation. Then only shall we enjoy any real serenity.

How far Lawrence evaded this obligation is a difficult question which I have no space to deal with here. But that that eloquent and imaginative writer, Mr Powys, is attempting to do so there can be little doubt.* His exultant Paganism is irrelevant to the adventure of the modern consciousness. This is clear enough from the fact that the centre of his Universe is still the personal self. It may be a very mature self, but it is still a self. Its aims are avowedly hedonistic: it is determined to reinforce its sense of individuality by feeling as intensely as it can. Since, as I say, it is a sophisticated self, it contrives to increase its vitality by deepening its experience

* His recent *In Defence of Sensuality* confirms this view.

of loneliness, by giving itself up to contemplation, by indulging in hate. But all the time it is drawing everything to the wrong centre. Further, in its attitude there is an element of definite perversity. For whereas Lawrence, as it were, boldly threw his intellect away, Mr Powys makes use of it in order to intensify the life of the senses. Which is simply sin.

But in any case the whole approach is wrong. To be reborn is to discover life again from the new centre of the One, to 'see the Sun in all things'. The senses and the emotions are not thereby deadened, but miraculously revivified. And this is the only path by which the modern civilized man will find his way back to tranquillity. It is the only fundamental solution of the 'Modern Dilemma'.

10. Literature, Sacred and Profane

The subtle fashion in which the possession of culture serves to prevent the individual from penetrating to the deeper levels of understanding is very well illustrated by our modern attitude to literature. I do not refer to that vast flood of letterpress which owes its genesis to vanity, commercial greed, or the search for sensation, but to what we are accustomed to describe as 'serious work'. How much of this 'serious work' is really justified? A far smaller amount, I suggest, than the majority of educated people are prepared to allow.

That there is a good deal of unnecessary writing the production of which is nevertheless excusable enough, one freely admits. To begin with, people need to earn their bread and butter, and they naturally, if they are sensitive, prefer to do so in some fashion which does not involve them in becoming cogs in the mechanism of commerce. For imaginative men and women today are deprived of those normal outlets for creative activity which have been destroyed by the universal mechanization of life.

They can no longer express themselves, as they should do, by making useful and beautiful objects, and they therefore achieve a partial satisfaction by writing novels and stories. Hence the remarkable amount of distinguished and sincere work which is appearing at the present time. The standard of execution is incredibly high; every month there appear a whole row of books, each of which represents the best which the talented author has in him (or her; particularly her).

I would submit, however, that just because the greater part of this writing is the expression of a creative impulse which has been deflected from its normal channel, it is lacking in true spiritual potency. No activity which is at bottom compensatory in character can produce really fruitful results. The novel which has really been written because its author has been deprived of the opportunity of motherhood, of working at a craft, or of finding satisfaction in religion, is not only superfluous, but also devoid of inseminating power. It is not for that particular individual a truly vital gesture.

Few realize this fact, for the reason that the writing of books happens today to have become a fashion. The gesture of authorship is accepted as being both natural and reasonable, and most of us do not pause to enquire what psychological significance it may possess. It is taken for granted that a young man is doing something meritorious in recording, and subsequently giving to the world, the ideas which he entertains about life. He is encouraged by publishers, critics, and public alike; the more fundamental problem of whether his activity is desirable in itself is hardly ever raised.

I suggest that it ought to be raised, and this even more in the case of the serious writer than in that of the manifestly commonplace individual. Is it not time that we considered the possibility that the vast majority of those people who sit down without compunction and without discouragement to 'express themselves' are really creating on the plane of imagination what they should properly create on the plane of life? Are they not, as it were, short-circuiting the flow of their vitality by resorting to symbolism when they should really resort to action? Are not their novels, plays, and short stories more than anything the results of a process of leakage, of a failure to achieve a true catharsis?

But what should such people *do*? There precisely lies the point. They have no idea in which direction to take action. So they talk, read, and write instead. And what they describe to us for the most part is that dreary and unintelligible world which exists for the individual who is still in a condition of internal division and confusion. True, the accounts which they give us of their experience are faithful enough. But it is a type of experience which is essentially insignificant. And it remains insignificant just because, through continually relieving the strain upon them by the act of writing, they never allow the tension within to become sufficiently powerful to bring about a deepening of consciousness. There is no restraint, so there is no profundity. The creative forces are never dammed up, and the lake as a consequence remains painfully shallow.

And now let us turn from these authors to their productions. It is pretty evident, I think, that the most distinctive note of modern letters is an uncompromising naturalism. The writer of today excels in depicting for us the stark realities of life, as they appear to the eye of the sincere and discerning observer, stripped of the veils which sentimentalism is ever ready to throw over them. The process is obviously extremely salutary. The atmosphere is cleared of those unhealthy vapours with which it was polluted in an earlier and less objectively minded age. We are at last presented with the facts, and presented with them in a remarkably complete fashion. There is honesty, there is singularly acute observation, there is terse and incisive statement, and particularly there are no false shrinkings and reluctances. The whole atmosphere is crisp, sparkling, antiseptic.

Now it may be argued with a good deal of justification that the modern author is really exercising the function of the artist in its most legitimate sense. He does not presume to judge; he only records—the process of recording entailing, of course, an act of creative selection. This was the view of Chekhov, expressed repeatedly in the course of his correspondence:

> Fiction is called artistic because it draws life as it actually is. Its aim is absolute and honest truth. To narrow its function to the special task of digging for 'pearls' is just as deadly for it as if you were to make Levitan paint a tree and ordered him not to include the dirty bark nor the yellow leaves. . . . The novelist's business is only to describe who has been speaking or thinking about God or pessimism, how, and in what circumstances. An artist must not be the judge of his characters or of what they say, but only an impartial witness. . . . You are right in demanding that an artist should take a conscious attitude to his work, but you confuse two conceptions: the solution of a question and the correct setting of the question. The latter alone is obligatory for the artist. . . . When I describe horse thieves, you would have me say: 'Stealing horses is evil'. But that was known long ago without me. Let the jury judge them; my business is simply to show what they are like.

The canons thus laid down by Chekhov are essentially the canons of modern art. And we cannot but be sensible of the sanity and objectivity which result. But at the same time we have to ask ourselves how far this resolute, unsentimental approach to experience can really aid us in dealing with our spiritual problems. Manifestly, naturalism is invaluable in its place: unless there is realism to begin with there is no sure foundation on which to build.

Our point of departure must be a wide-eyed recognition of the facts.

I suggest that we have by now reached a stage at which we have a sufficient knowledge of the facts. We do not know all the facts; their number is infinite. But we do know, thanks to the tireless curiosity of our inquisitorial modern writers, pretty exhaustively what life means for most types of human beings. The life of the poor and oppressed as it really is; the real emotions of the soldier in the trenches, of the abandoned mistress, of the disillusioned libertine, of the sexual pervert, of the successful man of business; the subtle fluctuations in the flow of sympathy between sensitive people; the infinite ways in which human beings can offend one another's susceptibilities; the particular shades of satisfaction and repulsion which are experienced by modern men and women in the course of their distraught and intricate lives—the catalogue is endless.

The survey is astonishingly complete, and its comprehensiveness and accuracy are largely due to the fact that our modern writers are deficient in true imaginative power. They are unable to create characters in the old, vigorous manner; nor would they if they had the capacity. So they content themselves with imparting to us instead an extraordinary amount of accurate information, obtained at first-hand. The transition is from poetry to science—and from one point of view we should be glad that it has taken place: our consciousness is being extended to a remarkable degree.

It is important to observe, however, that the extension is *horizontal*: we are being provided with a vastly increased number of facts, facts which have little significance until they have been interpreted. For until they are interpreted we shall remain overpowered by our bewildering modern experience. And in this connexion it is instructive to consider a further extract from Chekhov's letters, bearing in mind particularly the fact that, written as it was in 1892, it may reasonably be taken to represent his more mature attitude to the problem:

> Remember that the writers whom we call eternal or simply good and who intoxicate us have one common and very important characteristic: they get somewhere, and they summon you there, and you feel, not with your mind, but with your whole being, that they have a certain purpose and, like the ghost of Hamlet's father, do not come and excite the imagination for nothing. . . . The best of them are realistic and paint life as it is, but every line is permeated, as with a juice, by awareness of a purpose; you feel, besides life as it is, also life as it ought to be, and this captivates you.

Not 'life as it is', but 'life as it ought to be'. What I am suggesting here is that the modern educated person is inclined to mistake that horizontal extension of consciousness which is brought about by a study of modern letters for that vertical extension which is involved in true spiritual illumination. He does not sufficiently realize that he is being presented all the time with multitudes of facts, but with few principles. And this is, I think, sufficiently borne out by the fact that the man of today, although highly *cultured*—in the sense that he has a very full knowledge of what happens—is at the same time conspicuously untutored in the art of conducting his life. People today are aware to a remarkable degree of what it is that has to be dealt with, of what facts must be faced, but they are no less distinguished by their restlessness and impotence. Never, surely, has a generation been so incredibly well informed and yet so fatally lacking in wisdom.

Why does modern literature fail them in this respect? The answer can only be that the writer of today is interpreting life while still standing on life's level. He is the ordinary person become articulate—not to say vociferous. He is an expert in re-evoking for us states of mind, but they are the states of mind of human all-too-human men and women. He enables us to see them clearly, but to see them only as they see themselves.

As a result the more exacting among us are becoming a little weary of reading his works. They have by this time had a surfeit of impersonal reporting, clinical observation, and factual description; they want to be given standards by which they can live. And they consequently turn instead to the work of the great writers of the past, of those men who enjoyed an 'awareness of purpose'. But how much real *moral* guidance will they obtain even from this source?

That 'pure' art can give them little assistance in this matter is fairly clear. The function of the pure artist, as Mr Middleton Murry rightly insists, is to reproduce for us the essences of objects. He presents us with human experience in its purity, so that we become familiar, if we are sufficiently sensitive, with the inner, distinctive character of the different modes of our being. Under the spell of his art we rise to contemplation and as a result we are spiritually refreshed. But although the supreme artist may in this fashion aid us in clarifying our experience, he is not concerned with telling us what we should *do*; he is not a therapeutist; he reveals to us the true nature of life—though evidently on an infinitely higher level than do the observers of its merely external features.

Of course, when the object of the artist's attention happens to be his own moral struggles he can manifestly aid us to a marked degree. We learn from such writers as Dostoevsky, Nietzsche, or D. H. Lawrence what man is really like, what he discovers when he dares to look resolutely into his own depths, when he makes a sincere effort to integrate his being. But these heroic spirits cannot lead us beyond the point which they have themselves attained. And that point is not by any means so remote as many of our literary hero-worshippers would have us believe. The fact remains that the greater number of those writers who have spoken with such magnetic power to the modern mind were personally moral failures. Tolstoi, Strindberg, Ibsen, Chekhov, Dostoevsky, Amiel —can it be said that any of these men, remarkable as they were, succeeded in resolving the discords within their being? Does not the fascination of studying their works lie largely in trying to discover where exactly it was that the indisputable breakdown occurred? No, their significance for us is to be found rather in the courage they displayed in laying bare the nature of the issues which are involved in man's attempt to unify his being. For they were all truly exposed to temptation, they all genuinely strove to resist temptation, and although they none of them attained to complete liberation, they succeeded at least in throwing a piercing light upon the dark places in the tortured modern soul. But it remains true that even in the case of these great figures we are still concerned with the plane of the actual rather than with the plane of the ideal, with what human beings are, as opposed to what they might become.

The superiority of such men lies more than anything in the scale on which they were built. They represented the weak, sinful, aspiring mortal writ large. They lived essentially *ici bas*, striving with the rest of us to attain to spiritual integrity. They had all the human passions in a supreme degree, and their feet were firmly planted on the earth. Hence they were able to speak to us in terms of our familiar, earthly experience, to describe their struggles, in vivid, objective form. They could bring the vital issues home to us with unparalleled force. Our debt to them is therefore incalculable.

There comes, however, a certain point at which we need the services, not of the chained Titan, but of a more pure, even though a less dynamic, type of spirit. We want someone who by the very nature of his being can confirm us in our more lofty and transient realizations, reinforce our weak and uncertain aspirations, recall to us the existence of a peace which passeth all understanding. And in this matter we turn instinctively to the individual who seems rather to have come down into the flesh from above than to be straining upwards to free himself from its limitations. In other words, we turn to the enlightened spiritual teacher, the prophet, the priest. For these people are by nature set apart. They are so constituted that they are at home in that strange region of being which for the passionate, doubt-ridden mortal is almost a distant dream; they know intimately a purity and a peace which the ordinary human being can realize only intermittently and precariously; they have a firm grasp of principles which the mass of men find to be at once authoritative and difficult to understand. In a word, they are concerned with the sphere of the sacred.

And the sphere of the sacred is not merely different from the quotidian and the passionately 'human'; it is positively hostile to it. It is a sphere in which the natural man feels uneasy, impotent, and unclean, a sphere in which the light seems to emanate from an unfamiliar quarter of the heavens. To dwell in it is to inhabit a Universe the centre of which is not self, but the One.

It is not going too far to suggest that every individual who pursues his search for spiritual illumination with sufficient persistence finally finds himself obliged to leave secular literature behind him. The divine as it is glimpsed from a distance by the earth-bound giant is not enough for him. He must sit at the feet of those who, even if they are less sympathetic figures, owe their authority to the fact that they are standing on more elevated ground. He must study *scripture*, a type of utterance which comes from a centre different from that from which the corrupted mortal is speaking.

The sacred is not to be confounded with the secular

word. It is not aspiring upwards, but bringing the light downwards to earth. I am not arguing here in support of the conception of revelation. I mean only that 'sacred' literature bears a distinctive stamp. It is written by men when they are in a peculiar condition, by men who have turned their backs on the world. And it affirms the existence and significance of a state of being which is foreign to that in which men normally find themselves. It emphasizes uncompromisingly the ideal instead of the actual; it evokes an atmosphere which is not evoked by other types of writing. And it expounds a wisdom which is not of this world.

People do not read this sacred literature today: they are too 'emancipated'. Or, at the most, they consider it as art—*i.e.,* in so far as it has a secular significance. The matters of which it treats are unreal to them. They will read Dostoevsky with avidity—chiefly because he lived a large part of his time in Hell, with the topography of which they are themselves perfectly familiar. But they forget that Dostoevsky himself was a passionate student of the New Testament. They are sensationalists; they want strong, rich meat, and find the dry bread of true spiritual teaching unassimilable. Yet I am bold enough to suggest that they will discover in the end that they cannot afford to dispense with it, and I think that the extremely cautious tributes of some of our more imaginative critics to the importance of 'High Religion' can be seen to point in this direction. They will come to realize at last that it is only by looking upwards that man can obtain light.

11. Culture and Cultus

I should like to conclude this long chapter by calling attention to a negative aspect of the modern cultural problem: the serious deprivation which is undergone by a generation which is unable to express its deeper realizations in dynamic terms.

Let us face resolutely the fact that the spiritual life of the great mass of cultivated people today is to a dangerous degree *passive*. They read books, sometimes to an audience, but chiefly in solitude; they frequent concerts and art exhibitions; they enjoy the experiences of travel and social intercourse. And, unless they belong to that minority which is endowed with talents, their attitude is all the time primarily receptive and self-regarding. They have perfected their sensibilities to a wonderful degree, but they are provided with no adequate outlet for discharging the emotion which has been induced by their response to the things of the spirit. There is an enormous amount of absorption, but little of that outgoing by which it should properly be balanced. And the consequence is a profound spiritual *malaise*.

Now there are excellent psychological reasons why the normal channel of expression for elevated emotion should be that of religion. For we are met with the principle that feeling seeks to discharge itself on the same level on which it has been generated. The effect of sublime music, of fine poetry, of great natural beauty, of human association on its more lofty levels, is that of awakening in us a consciousness of the Infinite. We find ourselves in a peculiar condition of tension and exaltation which is not to be relieved by any ordinary type of behaviour. We are lifted out of the system of our normal everyday relationships and are denied the usual means of expressing our feelings. The organism is highly charged with electricity and is provided with no proper channels along which that electricity can be conducted. The result is more often than not a passing over into an unhealthy condition of mind. And the reason is simply that the only object which is really adequate to satisfy the soul when it is in this particular state is a supernatural object: that of the

Divine. It is only by bringing into association the negative process of being stimulated and the positive process of pouring out the heart in an act of devotion to Something completely transcendental in character that such rapture can be really safely experienced. It is only through this process that a true catharsis can be achieved.

But the effect which great beauty has upon us today is in a large measure that of exasperating our nerves, of making us restless and ultimately miserable. For we are paying the penalty for dissociating the beautiful from the moral—as Tolstoi, to the indignation of the cultured, so clearly pointed out in his *What is Art?* We abstract from a Mass its purely musical content, we read the Bible for its literary appeal, we treat ecclesiastical architecture and painting as if it were secular, concerning ourselves in every case with our purely æsthetic relationship to the object. And yet all the time we have within us a starved impulse towards religious devotion, which is never satisfied organically with our thirst for beauty. Unless, indeed, we sneak round to Westminster Cathedral in a wistful attempt to recall to ourselves the profoundly satisfying experience of blending sensuous pleasure with aspiration and love.

Another unsatisfactory feature of the condition of most cultured people today is that their spiritual life has no real point of focus. Both in its negative and its positive aspects it is diffuse to an inordinate degree. There are moments of elevation, inspired by a sunset, a page of Blake, a Mozart quartet, or a beautiful human contact. And there are irregular movements of spiritual outgoing. But there is no rhythm, no centrality, no concentration—and, above all, no discipline. It is altogether a touch-and-go affair, determined by the vicissitudes of the daily life. As a consequence, there is a notable instability and an inner sense of impoverishment and dissatisfaction. The individual is all the time living from hand to mouth.

One perceives here the tremendous deprivation which is undergone by the person for whom definite religious faith and practice are no longer possible. As there are no rites and ceremonies in which he can participate, he loses the enormous privilege of associating his physical body with his most profound states of mind. He has no means of unifying the æsthetic and the devotional elements in his soul. There is no institution in his private life for regularly bringing his thoughts back to a centre from which he can derive sustenance and power, no routine for reinforcing his flagging aspirations and resolutions. He has no means of symbolizing the unity of all in the One in terms of physical association. He never has the privilege of attending a gathering which is specifically sacred in character, which is held in a place set apart from other places, in which not only the interior aspect of the building but everything which takes place therein symbolizes the fact that the ordinary worldly state of mind has been momentarily forgotten; in which those present are not simply associated together, but united in Something which transcends them all.

This last point is of great significance. Our modern romantics are rediscovering the importance of living in the Unity. The realization is of incalculable moment. But it cannot escape our attention that up to the present they only concern themselves with apprehending that unity in purely contemplative terms—each one sitting alone in his room reading Keats, or listening to the gramophone. But any mode of expression which is to be at all satisfying must involve *action*. And to express one's sense of unity in terms of action means something more than being charitable and tolerant to those with whom one comes in contact, or bestowing one's approval on movements which make for the breaking down of cultural and economic barriers. It means what Americans call 'getting together'.

But it is a notable fact that the modern cultivated person shrinks from such a prospect with dismay. He does not mind realizing the Whole in terms of poetic appreciation, but he is horrified at the thought of expressing it in terms of flesh and blood. For one thing he would immediately become terribly self-conscious—a clear indication that the impulse towards unity is still very weak. Yet I will not hesitate to affirm that until our sick and sophisticated souls can contrive to pass from assimilating and analyzing to symbolizing Unity in a definite material form they will never regain their lost integrity. They are introverted to an abnormal degree; they have no outlet for that 'giving oneself away' which is the basis of all spiritual health. They are self-centred—not so much out of native indifference to association as because there does not exist for them any cause to which they can conscientiously dedicate themselves.

I suggest that the modern cultivated person is *over-estimating* his power of maintaining contact with the realm of the spiritual in his present condition. He begins, perfectly sincerely, by rejecting traditional religious beliefs, but forgets that those beliefs have served in the past as centres around which have been organized all manner of practices which were of immeasurable value from the point of view of spiritual hygiene. He imagines in his self-sufficiency that he can get along satisfactorily without rites and ceremonies, without private disciplines, without associating himself on a religious basis with a group of his fellow-men. But the plain fact is that he cannot—unless he is a very exceptional person indeed. The great mass of more highly educated men and women today—those anyway of a more spiritual type—are psychologically unstable, restless, unfulfilled, and morbidly self-conscious, and all this because they are attempting to reduce their transactions with life to purely æsthetic and humanistic terms.

I do not mean that in most cases there is any other course open to them. In declining to associate themselves with existing religious organizations of a traditional type they are, I am convinced, following a perfectly right instinct. For any individual who is truly possessed of the modern consciousness no other course is possible. The religion of the Churches is a dead religion; on that point one must remain firm. What I want to emphasize, rather, is the fact that it is little use for modern educated people to pretend that they can get along without *any* religion beyond the vague idealism of the cultured. Their lives have no secure spiritual foundation, and at heart they know that this is so—in spite of the Sense of the Whole and all the rest of it. And until some new Religion takes shape which will at the same time prove acceptable to their intelligences and provide them with a proper framework for their lives, they will remain, if they have been spiritually quickened, profoundly unhappy at heart.

CHAPTER VI

THE NEW ROMANTICISM

THE discussion of the cultural problem to which the last chapter was devoted will, I hope, have prepared the ground for an examination of the neo-romantic philosophy. For in the New Romanticism we are presented with an attitude to life in which the æsthetic element plays a part of the very first importance. And in order to understand that attitude with any completeness we shall be obliged to go still more thoroughly into the question of the use and abuse of the imaginative faculty.

In dealing with the new humanists I regarded myself as justified in restricting my attention to the work of the leading exponent of their ideas, Mr Irving Babbitt. In the same way, in considering the romantic point of view, I shall restrict my attention to the work of Mr Middleton Murry. For in the writings of that remarkable critic there is to be found at once the most eloquent, the most thoroughgoing, and the most audacious modern statement of the romantic philosophy.

Not that I have any wish to underrate the significance of the contribution made by Mr Fausset, from whose most valuable *Proving of Psyche* I have already made abundant quotation. But although he has given us an admirable exposition of the romantic standpoint, he is by no means a 'pure' romantic as Mr Murry may claim to be. For one thing, he is religious in a sense in which Mr Murry is not, and, for another, there are passages in his writings which go to suggest that he is not destined to remain satisfied for very long with an exclusively 'romantic' philosophy. But for Mr Murry it is romanticism first and last. And by the very uncompromisingness of his attitude he focusses the vital issues for us in a way in which Mr Fausset cannot.

Further, he has a legitimate right to be considered the leader of the modern romantic school. Both in his books and in his journal, the *Adelphi*, which he founded in June, 1923, and edited until June, 1930, he has defined the principles of the new faith with a persuasiveness and distinction which have inevitably won for his ideas a large number of sympathizers. In a word, the New Romanticism stands or falls with Mr Murry to the same degree that the New Humanism stands or falls with Mr Babbitt. I make no apology, therefore, for confining myself in this chapter to an analysis of his theories.

Such a procedure, it is to be admitted, entails certain disadvantages. The greater number of the ideas which he advances are accepted without reserve by the majority of the people who are today taking their stand upon this particular philosophy of life. Others, on the contrary, are peculiar to Mr Murry himself. One must not conclude, for instance, that every modern romantic is necessarily an atheist! Or, again, that his ideas regarding Jesus and Shakespeare meet with as wide an acceptance as do some of his others. But to differentiate between what is personal to the author of *God* and what is most broadly representative of the romantic movement would be to complicate the issues in an unnecessary and unprofitable fashion. Further, I cannot but welcome the opportunity of discussing Mr Murry's theories in some detail, for the reason that they have never yet, to my knowledge, been examined in any systematic way. And since on the one hand Mr Murry is probably the most important critic living in England today, and on the other it is now nearly eight years since the movement first began, the time would seem to be ripe for an examination of his ideas.

A word at the outset regarding the term 'romantic'. I am inclined to regard it as somewhat unfortunately chosen. It is a little too suggestive of revolt and extravagance, a little too provocative. And, strictly speaking, the neo-romantic is no more in revolt than is the new humanist—except in the sense that one is necessarily in revolt in repudiating the corrupt standards of one's time. Actually, the romantic stands for a sober, disciplined attitude of mind—although the fact may be by no means apparent to those who associate sobriety and discipline only with the acceptance of a rigid, traditional scheme. More important, however, is the fact that the central element in the romantic's position is the affirmation of the significance of a type of consciousness in which the 'romantic' and the 'classical' elements are perfectly balanced. This is brought out with exceptional clearness by Mr Fausset. And Mr Murry himself has made an admirable statement on the point in an article published in the *Monthly Criterion* (June, 1927) entitled 'Towards a Synthesis'. The choice of the word would seem, indeed, to have been determined less by a clear sense of the actual implications of the attitude than by the exigencies of controversy: the term offered itself only too readily as a point of focus for those who were engaged in opposing the neo-classicism of such writers as Mr Babbitt.

The point is, however, of minor importance. Let me turn to the philosophy itself. And here the first thing to realize is that, whatever reservations one may make regarding the soundness of the romantic attitude, one is obliged to take it with the utmost seriousness if one wishes to understand the deeper import of the crisis through which the modern consciousness is at present passing. In his quest for a satisfactory basis for life the man of today is presented first of all with the philosophy of scientific humanitarianism. He soon finds, if he is in the least imaginative, that it offers him no secure foundation for dealing with his experience. He is accordingly impelled to seek instead for some attitude to life which recognizes more adequately that the moral problem is in the last resort personal and private in character, to be resolved not from without, but by changing the nature from within. And this means that he will have to choose between those two philosophies which are at present represented by the respective standpoints of the new humanists and the new romantics—unless, of course, he compromises between them or achieves a synthesis of the two.

My reasons for concluding that the discriminating person will finally be led to abandon the attempt to live on 'classical' principles have already been laid before the reader: the essence of the matter is that Humanism fails to satisfy the 'heart'. The consequence is that the man or woman who has come to realize the shortcomings of that philosophy will almost inevitably become a convert to romanticism. Indeed, for the individual who has come to perceive where classical Humanism breaks down and who is at the same time incapable of religious faith in the traditional sense, no other alternative would seem to be possible. That is why the New Romanticism is winning the allegiance of some of the finest and most sensitive minds which we have among us today.

For it is essentially a *patrician* philosophy. Its appeal is to the elect, and to the elect alone. Not only has the enlightened romantic perceived the limitations of scientific humanitarianism, but he has also contrived—so far at least as the intellectual aspect of the problem is concerned—to embody in his outlook the virtues of the classicist while at the same time rejecting with decision the weaker elements in his position. He is not so foolish as to deny the claims of the calculating intellect, but he assigns to them their proper significance, perceiving with remarkable clearness that real illumination can only come from that act of imagination in which the head and the heart are working together in creative harmony.

As a result, his philosophy is distinguished by the fact that it does the most complete justice to the poetical element in our experience. It recognizes man for what he is: a creature who is not only rational, but is filled also with a deep and mysterious sense of the infinite, and who cannot be satisfied by any type of thinking which does not bring him into an imaginative relationship to it. The appeal which it exercises is therefore in a high degree æsthetic. The romantic does not merely attach due importance to the higher manifestations of imaginative thought; he constantly appeals to them in order to make clear the nature of the principles for which he stands.

Nor is this all. He is emphasizing all the time the importance of a type of experience which is religious in all but name. He is at home in that curious realm of thought in which the rationalist finds himself at sea and only the poet and the mystic are able to orientate themselves aright. And he reveals his deep insight into the moral problem by insisting on the fact that, in order to be at peace with the universe, a man must not merely discipline his passions but be born again. Is it any wonder, therefore, that he is being listened to today with an attentive ear?

And yet, while recognizing all this, I am venturing in what follows to put forward the view that Romanticism, although it represents a marked advance upon the position of the classical humanist, cannot really leave us satisfied. Although both profound and refined as a philosophy, it is not ultimate. It takes account of the findings of the heart in a manner which Humanism fails to do, but it interprets our experience too exclusively in naturalistic terms.

I have no intention of undertaking a detailed analysis of Mr Murry's philosophy. I shall limit myself for the most part to examining those of his ideas which serve to bring out most definitely the points at issue between him and the religious thinker. I shall then be in a position to consider the respects in which this purely 'humanistic' attitude to life breaks down in practice.

1. Metabiology

The reader may perhaps expect me to begin this study with a criticism of Mr Murry's system of 'Metabiology'. The only real justification for doing so would be that he was offering us something definitely new in the shape of a vitalistic philosophy. But I am obliged to confess that, although, as one would expect, in the course of developing his theme he has let fall by the way many extremely valuable ideas, his Metabiology does not seem to me to present any markedly original features. It is true that he has given the distinctive name of 'metabiological' to those variations—like, for instance, the *weltanschauung* of Plato—which are transmitted to posterity through the medium of consciousness rather than through physical reproduction, and treated their relationship to purely biological variations in a remarkably suggestive manner. But otherwise his attitude would appear to be substantially that of the ordinary vitalist. Admittedly, he alludes contemptuously to those people who believe in 'some mere Life-force which gives us all the excuse for doing merely what we want to', but the reason why his own 'World-organism' should be regarded as being essentially different in character continues to escape me.* We are Its instruments; through

* A more engaging monster than Mr Murry's 'World-organism' is the Life-force of Mr C. E. M. Joad (see his *Matter, Life, and Value*). Mr Joad is sufficiently receptive to the appeal of evolutionism to subscribe to the doctrines of Vitalism. Yet at the same time—and this is what makes his work significant for us today—he is so deeply stirred by the

us It ' strains after newness '. Yet at the same time ' we cannot say whether a Consciousness exists for which the totality of experience is present in its own immediate validity '. Certainly It has other than purely biological ends; but then so has any other reputable member of the species. For they all use as their ' instruments ', not only cats and dogs, but also artists, mathematicians, and poets, and in particular the authors of those treatises in which, as in Mr Murry's own, they elucidate to themselves the principles of their own behaviour.

Nor does the ' World-organism ' fail to raise for us the usual teleological problems. How, for example, unless self-consciousness was inherent in it from the beginning, did it come to be guided in its blind searchings to just that point at which self-consciousness appears? How can the individual, strictly speaking, be the ' instrument ' of something the character of which he modifies by the

---

conception of a timeless world beyond the flux that he will only tolerate the notion of a Life-force if it is conceived as achieving its final object by coming to rest in the contemplation of the Eternal and Supernatural. Clearly this is no real solution of the problem, for Mr Joad, being a determined pluralist, is totally unable to explain to us—in fact he does not make any serious attempt to do so—how it comes about that the urge within the entrails of the Life-force should impel it just in that particular direction and in no other. Such a magnetic pull exerted upon the temporal by the Eternal surely implies the existence of a unity underlying that duality on which he so implacably insists. It looks, indeed, as if he has mistaken a distinctness for analysis for a distinctness within reality. Instead of ' dividing in order to distinguish ' he has ' distinguished in order to divide '.

Not being a philosopher, I put forward these suggestions with the utmost diffidence. But it is at least plain to me that the appearance at the present juncture of such a hybrid product as Mr Joad's system points to a definite movement away from a philosophy of Flux.

very act of exercising that instrumentality? How if It expresses Itself through instruments which possess self-consciousness, personality, and will, can it fail to have these things Itself as Its minimum attributes? How can we believe that the whole exquisitely complex order of Nature was created by this Entity by an unconscious process, and that It only realized what It had done when It became aware of Itself in the minds of human beings? In fine, we meet with all the familiar difficulties which attend the attempt to explain life from below upwards instead of from above downwards.

2. Visible and Invisible

So much for Mr Murry's Metabiology. What I now wish to do is to draw nearer the problem with which we are particularly concerned by considering his extremely individual attitude towards the place of Mind in the Universe.

His point of departure is the fact that the testimony of the Mind as to the nature of life conflicts violently with that of the Heart. We can conceive of a harmonious order of being, but what we are actually confronted with is a painfully inharmonious order, an order in which the unjust prosper, in which genius is meaninglessly cut off in its youth, in which capacity is unrelated to opportunity. Between what the Heart responds to instinctively and what the Mind actually discovers there is a cruel and irresolvable contradiction.

The way in which Mr Murry deals with this contradiction is interesting: he concludes that it exists only in the order of consciousness and not in the order of reality. In the face of the problem the unaided mind is impotent:

> The more resolute romantic accepts the reality of the external universe, and finds the cause of its contradiction with

the internal world—a contradiction theologically expressed as the opposition of free-will and necessity—in a limitation of the human consciousness. He believes that the human consciousness has not yet reached the point in its own development where it is capable of truly apprehending reality; such a change he believes to be inevitable, and towards such a change he strives. (*God : An Introduction to the Science of Metabiology*, 1929, p. 54)

The first point to which I would call attention here is that, considered in conjunction with his idea of an evolving World-organism, Mr Murry's conception of the limitations of the rational mind raises for us peculiar difficulties. For it is one thing to lose faith in the intellect as a theist and quite another to lose faith in it as a vitalist. M. Shestov's irrationalism and alogism, for instance, may in many respects be very disconcerting to our minds. But they are not so disconcerting as Mr Murry's. According to the theological conception, the Consciousness for which the conflict between free-will and necessity is resolved is thought of as being *already in existence*; as we develop we enter into it in an increasingly complete fashion. In Mr Murry's views, on the contrary, it has not yet come into being; indeed it *cannot* have come into being. For if once it be allowed that there is somewhere or other a Consciousness which is *ahead* of that consciousness which is manifested by the collective mind of the Race, a Consciousness which is aware now of that which men and women will be aware of only at a later stage—then there is at once created a distinction between values and their embodiment which is fatal to his whole philosophical scheme. 'Values', he writes, 'are always incarnate and embodied; the "value" that is not incarnate is simply not a "value". The hypostatization and detachment of "values" from the organic process in which they emerge is an error'.

The only inference we can make, therefore, is that the

process of the Universe is somehow right in and by itself, even though it operates in a completely blind fashion. Let us say that the gradual unfolding of life is such that the state of affairs resulting will prove to be perfectly satisfying to man's unified consciousness when the time comes for him to develop it. Everything is essentially good, and this we shall one day come to see. Meanwhile, however, we have sinned. That is to say, we have fostered, or yielded to the temptation of fostering, a false, rational consciousness to which the Universe presents itself as containing evil and incomprehensible features.

Why a process of blind movement should culminate in the appearance of a self-consciousness which perceives that everything which was accomplished in blindness is valid and satisfying, must remain a mystery—a mystery which is certainly no more easy to accept than that entailed in the old-fashioned, discredited theory that the Universe was created by God. Further, it would be interesting to know how it came about that, in the course of its evolution, consciousness came to commit the crime of detaching 'values' from 'the organic process in which they emerge'. Was it overcome by 'the vast inertia which lurks for ever throughout the whole'? Or—which is always possible—will this apparent perversion be subsequently found by consciousness to have been a necessary stage in its development towards perfection? For if once you substitute for an Omniscient God a blindly infallible Tendency in Life, and assume, further, that consciousness will in time come to realize the nature of that tendency—then clearly any apparently disastrous state of affairs may prove to have been wisely determined from the beginning. In fact, the person who believes that, in spite of all appearances, the World-organism is really behaving itself properly, stands in relation to It in very much the same position as the religious person does to his God.

It knows best; in the end we shall discover that even though It was blind It was rightly inspired.

But I will not pursue these speculations further here. Let us return to the question of the limitations of the human intellect. In a passage very similar in purport to that which I have already quoted, Mr Murry writes in the following terms:

> The object concerning which the Heart and Mind are in discord is the moral nature of the Universe. The conclusions of the Mind concerning the moral nature of the Universe are such that they afford no satisfaction to the Heart. In terms of the religious consciousness . . . this discord between Mind and Heart appears as a consuming desire of the Heart 'to know God', which is absolutely disappointed by the Mind's deliverance that the world manifests no sign of the existence of a just, far less of a loving, God. (*God,* p. 124)

That the problem of religion is essentially the problem of resolving the contradiction between the inside and the outside of life, between what presents itself to the extraverted mind and what is discovered within by the introverted 'heart', is clearly true. Up to this point one is prepared to accept Mr Murry's description as accurate enough. What one questions, however, is his limited conception of the capacities of the reason. It seems impossible not to conclude that he has dispensed with its services at too early a stage, and that, with a thoroughly 'romantic' gesture, he is mystically submitting himself to an irrational Universe which is in reality very much more rational than he would have us suppose.

Take first the conclusions to which the Mind is led as a result of contemplating the wider processes of Nature. According to Mr Murry, they yield no evidence of the existence 'of a just, far less of a loving, God'. Actually, of course, Mr Murry does not believe in the existence of *any* sort of God, just or unjust. What reply can the religious thinker make to such assertions?

Well, there is little that can be said. It is freely recognized by theologians that, although it is the *experience* of the religious man that Nature reveals God, any attempt to *deduce* His existence from the character of the natural world can at the best only hope for a very limited degree of success. To the individual who is not illuminated it will necessarily present itself as a realm of conflict and meaningless change. Yet it remains true that the Argument from Design, whether it be formulated in strictly logical terms, or whether it presents itself in an unorganized but impressive form to the mind of the ordinary reflective person, does have a certain weight. It is difficult not to allow that the Universe does possess characteristics which point to its creation by a wise Intelligence. And one cannot but believe that most people at heart are inclined to accept this conclusion.*

What inspires one to protest, however, is the fact that Mr Murry, like so many other modern critics, tacitly assumes that this type of evidence has no longer any significance for us. There is a curious convention in existence that certain conclusions are unacceptable to the 'modern

* The fact that, according to certain modern theories of physics, the basis of the whole structure may be 'illogical' does not really affect the validity of the argument. For, however capricious and unpredictable the behaviour of electrons may be, it remains true that the outcome of their activity is a Cosmos within which events take place in such a way as to justify the belief of science in the principles of the uniformity of Nature.

Nor is the force of the argument diminished on the assumption which is made by some Eastern philosophers that the world is nothing but *maya*. For although on this view all is illusion, it is an ordered universe which constitutes the illusion; not a chaos. The Not-self is opposed to Brahman, yet its character is somehow determined by His perfection.

mind', although no really cogent reason is ever advanced as to why this should be so. Yet it is doubtful whether the recent discoveries of science have not tended to strengthen, rather than weaken, the case for the probability of God's existence.

But our chief concern, after all, is with the personal fate of the individual. Even if I accept the general scheme as being an expression of the will of God, it still remains to me a deep mystery why I should be destined to play one part in the drama rather than another. Science may demonstrate to me up to a point that I owe my tuberculosis and partial blindness to certain hereditary influences, but I still require to know why it is I rather than A or B who should be marked out as an invalid.

And here, it is plain, reason can offer us little aid. We are thrown back upon Faith. If we are vaguely religious we hold fast to the belief that the contradiction between freedom and necessity is somehow resolved in the heart of Reality. If we are theists we say that we are all the time in the hands of a merciful and wise God: 'Are not two sparrows sold for a farthing? And one of them shall not fall on the ground without your Father'.

What it is important to observe, however, is that the religious person does not thereby relinquish his belief in the rationality of the Universe. True enough, he is only too ready to allow that at a certain point the discursive mind simply fails us. Directly we become concerned with the really fundamental issues we are dependent upon the 'wisdom of the heart', upon our intuitions, upon our immediate, internal consciousness of reality. The *ultimate* explanation of all things must remain utterly hidden from our understanding. We have no idea why the sky should appear to us as blue, why one flower should be red and another white, why seeds grow into plants, why we are driven to recognize that one link in a chain of reasoning follows from another. *Omnia exeunt in mysterium.*

But this is not to say that all those processes which we fail to comprehend are on that account deemed to be irrational. We have the good sense to suspend our judgment. There is a God who makes all things work together for good. We assume—and in this matter the religious person is standing on exactly the same ground as the more imaginative secular thinker—that in our present condition we 'see through a glass darkly' and 'know in part'. There must always be mysteries. But, as we develop, the deeper implications of the scheme will, we hope, gradually reveal themselves to us.

This, however, is very far from being the attitude of Mr Murry. In his *God* we meet with the following confession:

> But to me they [these words of Keats'] have always meant a lucid ecstasy of self-immolation before the blind and beautiful power of Necessity, an almost exultant acceptance of the wreck of hope, a stab of pain, and a thrill of pleasure in the single act of pressing home to one's soul the bitterness of human destiny. (p. 21)

The impression made upon the mind by this extraordinary passage cannot but be disquieting. We feel on the one hand that there is a profound virtue in this unqualified submission to Life, a submission which is infinitely more complete and significant than that involved, for instance, in the passionless resignation of the Stoic. But we are no less sensible of the fact that Mr Murry has in some fashion misrepresented our relationship to Necessity for the sake of extracting a voluptuous and perverse sensation from abandoning himself to it. The situation is, in fact, 'romantic' in the most dangerous sense. We are impelled to reconsider the problem in a more tranquil frame of mind.

At the beginning of this enquiry we accepted Mr Murry's conclusion that the Heart and the Mind were in conflict regarding the moral nature of the universe. Looking more closely, we perceive that it is not actually the Heart and Mind, but rather *the reason* and *the senses*, which thus find themselves opposed. For, in the first place, that desire of the Heart of which he speaks is clearly a desire for justice and rationality: otherwise the Heart would not be so disappointed at the Mind's deliverance that these qualities are so imperfectly expressed in the phenomenal world! And, in the second place, it is not the Mind which causes this dilemma, but the data which are provided for it by the senses. It is upon the evidence of the senses that the Mind is led to conclude that the world cannot possibly have been created by a wise and merciful God.

The religious experience is the experience of reconciling this opposition. The individual attains to the realization that beneath the visible diversity there lies an invisible unity; and he therefore finds himself able to accept the world. But he does not as a result sacrifice the principle of rationality. What he sacrifices is the realm of appearances, and this by affirming that if it denies the reality which he is inwardly able to conceive, this is because it is imperfect, a part only of a wider whole. In other words, he holds on to reason and justice in the face of the evidence of his senses.

Mr Murry exactly reverses this process. To begin with he has passed through a genuine mystical* experience; he

* It is a matter of regret to me that in this chapter, as indeed throughout the book, I have been obliged to make use of the terms 'mystic' and 'mystical'; it would probably be an advantage if they were done away with altogether. Anyway, I should like to make it clear that I am concerned here with the mystic, not in so far as he is a person who on occasion enjoys visions and ecstasies, but in so far as he realizes

has apprehended the fact that beneath the duality there lies a unity, and that that unity is perfectly satisfying to the soul. That this is indeed the case no person who has any first-hand knowledge of the mystical can possibly doubt. But at the same time it is no less obvious that he is temperamentally a poet—and the mark of the poet is that he apprehends the Real, not inwardly, but as it is manifested in the forms of the phenomenal world. And this signifies again that his spiritual experience is intimately bound up with the life of his senses.

When, therefore, Mr Murry attains to a vision of the mystical we find that, instead of sacrificing his senses to his reason, he sacrifices his reason to his senses! Instead of concluding that his inner feeling of the validity of reason and justice must be trusted in spite of the objective evidence to the contrary, he concludes that the desire for these things is merely an expression of the frailty of the human heart, and that the world of our actual experience is the true reality:

> There is, it is true, a deep-rooted human instinct demanding that the world shall satisfy our hearts. . . . The man who has not felt the longing can scarcely be called a man. But why should it be satisfied? There is no reason save the desire of the human heart. (*New Adelphi,* III, ii, 118)

From this position two results follow. In the first place, the reason ceases to have any function in bringing us into relation with reality. A distinction is established between the 'practical consciousness' which 'aims at making reality amenable' and the 'imaginative consciousness' which attends to things 'for what they are'. And this second consciousness is by definition irrational;

---

the divine in terms of his personality—the religious man, in fact, at his highest. But to have abandoned the terminology actually employed would have been to complicate the issues to an undue degree.

for 'the unity of the universe is biological, not logical'. (*God*, p. 249) We can only apprehend the Real by leaving our rational minds behind us. Hence also all action is devoid of spiritual significance; it is essentially an activity of the 'practical consciousness'. The Real is only attained to by contemplation.

In the second place, it is to be concluded that the world revealed to us by the senses is essentially good. It can only appear unsatisfying to the mind which has failed to become properly imaginative. True religion consists in seeing 'things as they are'. If they outrage our sense of truth and beauty, this is because we have not yet learned to submit ourselves mystically to life. The profound spiritual principle that the Good is not completely such until it has become outwardly manifested is thus converted by Mr Murry into the principle that everything which is outwardly manifested is on that account good! The visible, instead of the invisible, becomes the criterion of reality. Everything is 'valid'—but incomprehensibly so. The apparently irrational must not be conceived as being merely the partially understood. There is no suggestion that the sphere of causality might possibly extend beyond the sphere of the visible, that if only we knew more facts what now appears as meaningless might become clear. No; everything must be justified purely mystically; what is apparently evil must be transformed into good by the contemplative eye. The realm of the sensible has at all costs to be rendered satisfying to the soul, however extreme the contradictions which it may contain. What takes place is right—but with an unaccountable rightness which the mind cannot fathom.

It need scarcely be said that the strain upon the individual who attempts to base his life upon such a topsy-turvy philosophy is extremely severe—hardly less so, in fact, than that imposed upon the Christian Scientist who clings at all costs to the belief that matter is unreal. What is called for is nothing less than a violation of the normal processes of consciousness. And we do not fail to detect in Mr Murry's writings evidence of the price which he is paying for following this particular road. That 'desire of the human heart' of which he speaks is not to be thwarted with impunity—for the good reason that it is nothing else but an urge towards the Real. Hence we continually find in writers of this tendency a persistent, if largely unconscious, attempt to re-introduce values into the substance of Reality, to find, after all, an ultimate justification for those deep interior convictions the validity of which they have denied. We are not surprised, therefore, to meet in Mr Murry's pages with such passages as the following (he is commenting upon Tchehov's beautiful observation that 'all things are forgiven, and it would be strange not to forgive'):

> 'All things are forgiven'. But by whom? Not by Tchehov. And hardly by God, in whom Tchehov did not believe in the ordinary sense of the word. But this pinnacle of consciousness was for him suprapersonal. It was not that he, Anton Tchehov, forgave all things. Not that at all. What he did was to feel and to know, in an awareness of a universal forgiveness, that it would be strange for him not to forgive. (*New Adelphi,* II, iv, 324)

Superficially regarded, this may seem to be one of the most fatuous statements which have ever come from the pen of a serious critic. Forgiveness which is not exercised by some sort of agent is a pure chimæra. But in the light of the foregoing it becomes readily comprehensible. Mr Murry's philosophy does not permit him to credit the World-organism with personality. But he is, nevertheless, impelled to endow It with human feelings: the Heart cannot indefinitely endure the misery of being alienated from the Real.

The same condition of interior discord finds expression

no less decisively in the general tone of Mr Murry's writing. In reading his pronouncements we are conscious all the time of a hysterical tendency, of a curious sort of *desperation*, suggesting irresistibly that he is attempting to fortify himself with a belief which is really too extreme to win his allegiance. Through taking the part for the whole and then proceeding to idealize it, he has become faced with the obligation of 'accepting' an intolerably irrational world. And this cannot but make for a profound internal distress. But such must inevitably be the result of passing through the mystical experience and yet resolutely refusing to recognize the existence of a supernatural.

3. Essential and Transcendental

As a result of the very individual position which he has taken up with regard to the significance of the mystical experience, Mr Murry, as will be clearly evident, finds himself committed to an uncompromisingly naturalistic philosophy. He does not, of course, make any attempt to deny the reality of the spiritual, but he seeks to describe it in rigorously non-transcendental terms. It is his belief that both the poet and the mystic are concerned with the Real, but he insists on the fact that there is absolutely no element of the supernatural in their experience. The vision of the seer is a vision of essences; Mr Murry follows faithfully here in the footsteps of Mr Santayana. Any beauty, truth, or goodness which is possessed by the objects in the world is not to be derived from their participation in anything beyond themselves, but is essential to them. The following passages should make his position clear to the reader:

But the absolute condition of the kind of thinking upon which we are embarked is that the subject of our thinking belongs wholly to the natural order. We suffer no taint, no magic or miracle to impoverish the richness of our theme. (*God,* p. 101)

To introduce, or to be prepared to introduce, the category of the supernatural into my thinking would be mental and spiritual suicide. (p. 112)

All pure phenomena are incomprehensible when viewed by the contemplative vision; but this universal incomprehensibility belongs to no one phenomenon more than to another. Moreover—and this is all-important—this universal incomprehensibility of things is absolutely compatible with their appearing natural. The identification of the incomprehensible and the unnatural is the error of Orthodoxy; the true identification is of the incomprehensible and the natural. (p. 89)

Once this position is accepted it necessarily follows that the notion of the existence of God is delusive:

God . . . is only an imaginary perfection of the Consciousness which, so far as we can know, glows into lucid flame in the human mind alone. (*New Adelphi,* II, iv, 327)

The personality and the love of God are, for the grown mind, only metaphors. (*Things to Come* (1928), p. 222)

God . . . is an intellectual and an imaginative fiction, necessary, as we have tried to show, as a medium for intellectual response to the variations in which the values he incorporates once actually emerged. . . . The mist of God disperses to reveal the wonder of the things that simply are. . . . God does not exist; but we shall never be able to do without him, unless we know in ourselves the reasons why he was created. (*God,* pp. 212, 282, 233)

At the same time the so-called mystical experience is inevitably conceived of in purely naturalistic terms:

Now precisely what has been hitherto lacking to every attempt at a complete Naturalism is a valid explanation of the mystical experience. . . . If we have been able to bring the mystical experience, without distortion or diminution, into harmony with a complete Naturalism, we may by an accident of experience have been able to succeed where others have failed. (*Ibid.,* p. 190)

Thus, on the third level, the mystical certainty is re-established. On the third and final and completely naturalistic level it runs thus: There is organic unity attainable by man, and there is an organic unity in the Universe, and the organic unity of man cannot be maintained without a knowledge of the organic unity of the universe. Less dazzling, perhaps, than the blinding certainty of the reality of the Soul and of God, yet not alien and remote from it; indeed, its direct and sole ancestry. (*Ibid.*, p. 169)

In considering the above passages we must begin by taking note of the fact that, in thus associating Romanticism with an uncompromising Naturalism, Mr Murry is following a path which is largely his own. We owe to the author of *God* some of the most illuminating statements to be found in modern literature regarding the nature of that unified consciousness to which both the romantic and the mystic attach such significance. But whereas a recognition of its importance does not necessarily involve a writer like Mr Fausset in the acceptance of a purely naturalistic philosophy, while for the mystic such a course is manifestly out of the question, for Mr Murry the two conceptions are inseparable, not merely organically connected, but complementary aspects of the same truth.

It is this conclusion which I am concerned to oppose here. I believe, on the one hand, that Mr Murry, in emphasizing the need for a deeper type of awareness, is stressing a truth of incalculable importance for the present generation; but I believe, on the other, not only that his naturalistic philosophy has its roots in a lower order of inspiration, but that a man by taking his stand upon 'romantic' principles is not on that account committed to accepting its tenets.

And in any case the position of the naturalist can scarcely be expected to impress any really unprejudiced mind. For we are again involved in that process of *localizing the issues* of which, as we saw in an earlier chapter, the classical humanist is also guilty, though in a very different fashion. In the case of Mr Murry, what we are met with is the assertion that in our transactions with the so-called spiritual there is nothing more entailed than a purely *natural* situation. What he would urge is that the mystics have *misinterpreted* their experience; they have mistaken what is really a penetration into the realm of essences for a penetration into something that lies beyond the natural altogether:

> What the mystical experience has to tell us is not, as is generally averred, the reality of God. That proposition is only an *interpretation* of the mystical experience, an interpretation which, it is true, is often given by the mystics themselves, because many of them were religious before they were mystics. But a non-religious mystic . . . will use quite different terms. (*New Adelphi,* I, ii, 105)

In other words, the mystics have read into the experience something that is not really there; their conception of God becomes what William James described as an 'over-belief'. Well, the only answer that one can make is that the same type of charge can equally reasonably be made against Mr Murry himself. The *fact* is that in our more elevated moments we find that the objects around us have become transfigured; we rise above the temporal into the region of the Eternal. We can then either say, with Mr Murry, that we have contrived for a space to see things 'as they really are', or we can say, with the mystics, that we have looked through them, as it were, into the being of that God Whose presence they reveal, that we have risen to the contemplation of that spiritual reality of which they are the vehicle or the reflexion. The beauty of the rose, the quality in a human voice, the sweep of the hills, then move us because we have pierced to the eternal life of which they are the transient embodiments.

Now I have no wish to argue here that this second interpretation is any more valid than the first. The point for us is that, taking the experience simply as a *datum of consciousness*, there is absolutely no way of proving that one is any more true than the other. A thing is changed into something other than its ordinary self. We can account for that change by saying that we have gained a vision of its 'essence', or by saying that we have perceived it in its transcendental aspect. But in either case the additional element which is perceived is something beyond the habitual. And just because it is beyond the habitual we have no way of determining in what its unwonted character consists. It is just as reasonable to charge Mr Murry with envisaging the transcendental in the limited terms of the natural as for him to charge the transcendentalist with introducing an unnecessary category into the equation. For there is no way of showing that what he describes in limited terms as the region of 'essences' is not the Divine in so far as it is immanent, in so far as it enters into the natural as a transfiguring influence. On that plane of the phenomenal to which Mr Murry restricts his attention no decision on the matter can in the nature of things be possibly reached. To deny the existence of the metaphysical on the grounds of purely physical evidence is, indeed, palpably a hopeless proceeding.

Nor do we become disconcerted when Mr Murry urges that by adopting this particular view he has 'simplified the calculus', and that his interpretation 'satisfies the law of intellectual economy'. Of course it does—in a sense. It is economical to explain the nature of consciousness, as the nineteenth-century physicists did, in terms of the motion of particles of matter. It is economical, again, to explain it, as the modern behaviourists do, in terms of purely physiological changes. But this is not to say that the resulting explanation is ultimate. Clearly it is economical to say that the conception of the supernatural is unnecessary and that we are concerned with nothing more than the essential. And if it is actually true that there *is* nothing more than the essential, then you have effected a very valuable economy indeed, by eliminating the superfluous conception of the divine. But if, on the other hand, it is actually true that what the naturalist describes as the essential is really God in so far as He is immanent in the world, then you have effected a simplification of a very different order—that simplification which is achieved when an object which has three dimensions is conceived of as if it had only two. Which view is the right one is not now the point: the point is that in neither case is any purely intellectual demonstration of the truth possible.

And, in any case, Mr Murry's contention that the mystics have misinterpreted the nature of their vision is extremely difficult to justify. It is true enough that when people entertain very definite ideas regarding the nature of God and our relationship to Him they tend very easily to explain their emotional experiences in theological terms. But it is also true that men and women undergo a distinctive type of experience—the experience, I mean, of *seeing the object as divine*. There is here no question of interpretation, for interpretation involves of necessity an act of retrospection. What is now involved, however, is not *retro*spection but direct *in*spection: a seeing-into the deeper nature of the object before them, a recognition that it is of God.

The character of this in-spection is, needless to say, impossible to describe to those who have not experienced it. But there exists a mass of testimony in favour of the conclusion that, in brief periods of ecstasy, men have seen Nature under its aspect of the garment of God, the showing forth in space and time of the immanent divine—however one cares to put it. Mr Murry, however, declines to make any distinction between a vision of 'essences' which is experienced solely as a revelation of beauty and truth, and a vision of 'essences' which is experienced as a revelation of the indwelling God. He claims, therefore, that Shelley's condition of reverie, in which one's being is 'dissolved into the surrounding universe', is identical with that known to the mystics. It is *not* identical, for the reason that in Shelley's experience there is lacking that integral element in the true mystical vision which consists in the consciousness that one is looking through Nature into God.

Now here, again, I make no attempt to urge upon the reader that the vision of the mystic is more ultimate than that of the poet. I wish only to stress the fact that Mr Murry is misrepresenting the true nature of the case. People, whether or not they are at the time in a state of delusion, do undergo this type of experience, and the fact must be accepted. As to its evaluation—that is altogether another matter. Since intellectual proof is entirely out of the question, we are obliged to fall back upon our immediate sense of quality. And once we find ourselves in this subjective region, Mr Murry's interpretation must be regarded as being no more compulsive than any other. In so far as the determining factor is feeling, there is no more to be said.

Nor is the position any different if we consider, instead, the mystic's *retrospective* evaluation of his experience. We are met with the fact that throughout the centuries the contemplation of the 'essential' has produced such a powerful effect upon the minds of certain men and women that they have been driven to infer that it must have its origin in something more ultimate than the natural. They have been led, by pondering upon their experience, to the conclusion that there exists a distinctively spiritual order, of which the natural is the reflexion.

Is this profound and recurrent feeling that there is something beyond the 'essential' the fruit of a less delicate type of discernment than that of the purely æsthetic observer who remains content with 'things as they really are', or is it not? Look at the problem how we will, it is certainly not to be resolved by the flat assertion that the first type of vision is merely of the order of illusion. One type of testimony must be taken as seriously as the other. Why should we be satisfied with Mr Murry's mere *assertion* that the experience of the supernatural is delusive? Is it not equally reasonable to maintain that his attempt to reduce it to purely æsthetic terms is an indication that his own insight is defective?

And one morning, as I was sitting by the fire, a great cloud came over me, and a temptation beset me; but I sate still. And it was said, 'All things come by nature'; and the elements and stars came over me, so that I was in a manner quite clouded with it. But inasmuch as I sate still and silent the people of the house perceived nothing. And as I sate still under it, and let it alone, a living hope arose in me, and a true voice, which said, 'There is a living God who made all things'. And immediately the cloud and temptation vanished away, and life rose over it all; my heart was glad, and I praised the living God.

So runs a notable passage in George Fox's *Journal*. What convincing reason has one to suppose that Mr Murry is right and Fox was wrong? How can we be sure that all of his ideas on this momentous question cannot be traced to some fundamental blindness of vision? It is simply one man against another.

The same problem of the relative value of conflicting testimonies is raised for us also by Mr Murry's characteristic treatment of the problem of 'conscience'. In an essay entitled 'The Creation of Conscience', published in the *New Adelphi* for December, 1929, he advances the view that conscience is nothing more than 'a sense of impending self-violation in a man if he performs certain acts'. It is perhaps better described, he would urge, as a sense of 'self-diminution': 'our private reluctances are our conscience'. There are, of course, many other points made in the article, but it is with the question of 'self-diminution' alone that we need concern ourselves here.

All I can say is that Mr Murry's handling of the question strikes me as being palpably inadequate. The real problem is not faced at all: it is not even raised. He has, in fact, resorted to that venerable device of the sophist which consists in presenting secondary, derivative aspects as if they constituted a total and satisfying account of a given situation. Obviously, when a man disobeys his 'conscience' he experiences a sense of 'self-diminution'. But the important point for us is: Why should the disregard of 'conscience' bring about this particular condition? Or, to put the matter in a different light, why should there be such a profound difference between a feeling of regret and a feeling of remorse? We do, or fail to do, certain things, and we become, as a result, deeply ashamed of ourselves. The experience is so universal, so fundamental, so difficult to explain in terms of simple fear or 'herd-instinct', that since the beginnings of civilization men have been driven to conclude that something far more radical is involved in the act of moral choice than is accounted for by the merely biological—or even metabiological—aspects of the case. The experience of sin, of alienation from a central source of goodness and truth, is so acute, so disproportionate to its immediate cause, that the fact of 'conscience' has become one of the most powerful of all agencies in inclining men's minds towards a spiritual explanation of the Universe.

On Mr Murry, it appears, it produces no such effect. Is this because he has succeeded in divesting it of an illusory glamour or because his 'conscience' happens to be weak? It is perfectly legitimate to assume that if its intimations became more insistent he would think differently. In a word, his testimony must take its place along with that of other men for whom the voice of 'conscience' has a different significance—the testimony, for instance, of such men as Baron von Hügel or Claude Montefiore, whose judgment in these matters cannot, to say the least of it, be regarded as being any less authoritative than Mr Murry's own.

4. The Problem of Evidence

There is, however, a more serious point to be considered. Mr Murry takes a certain satisfaction in describing himself as a 'hero worshipper'. And his greatest heroes are, as is to be expected, those men and women who have possessed that unified consciousness of which he has written so much. But the majority of them happen also to be people who believed with great earnestness in that divine order the existence of which he is so emphatic in repudiating. What, then, does he do? The answer is simple. He calmly assures us that, although they were inspired in so far as they were alive to the need to unite the head with the heart, they were deluded in so far as they held that there is anything above the plane of the natural. Jesus was a great prophet —up to the point where he expressed his belief in the existence of a Heavenly Father. Goethe was a profound spirit—though his references to an Almighty God, and his affirmation that *'Alles vergängliche ist nur ein Gleichnis'*, only go to indicate that he was not properly 'disintoxicated' of the transcendental. Coleridge had a deep insight into the more fundamental problems of consciousness—though he had not yet emancipated himself from the error of theism. And so on.

Now this seems to me to be perilously near intellectual dishonesty. Admittedly the vision even of the genius is markedly unequal in its penetration. Newton ceased to be Newton when he became concerned with problems of scriptural prophecy; Dostoevsky's politics were those of a conventional Slavophile. This we allow. But when it is a question of two such intimately related problems as that of the nature of consciousness and that of the character of the objects which are presented to it, we are bound to take a man's testimony all of a piece. To drop one half, as Mr Murry does, because it does not happen to square with his theories is palpably unjustifiable. If Coleridge's inner sense of the need to unify the being is to be regarded as significant, then his equally strong sense of the existence of a transcendental realm of spirit is to be regarded as significant also. Both are deliverances of the same consciousness, and in relation, moreover, to essentially the same issues. But Mr Murry would have us accept the idea that these thinkers were in the right whenever they spoke of the soul and in the wrong whenever they spoke of the metaphysical character of the phenomenal world. And against this procedure one must protest. If Goethe is worth listening to on the subject of the human spirit, he is equally worth listening to on the subject of God. And if Coleridge is to be regarded as speaking with authority on the nature of the poetic consciousness, he is to be regarded as speaking with authority also on the nature of the world of appearances. The Jesus, the Goethe, the Coleridge who exist simply for the purpose of confirming Mr Murry's ideas are nothing else but arbitrary abstractions unrelated to reality.

Nor is this all. Mr Murry not only ignores the fact that his heroes believe in the supernatural, but he even goes so far, on occasion, as to misrepresent seriously the position which they have taken up.

Take his treatment of Coleridge. In the course of a remarkable essay—remarkable, I mean, for the insight which it displays into the nature of the poetico-mystical consciousness—on the 'Philosophy of Poetry', he advances the contention that Coleridge shared his own belief in the unity of man with Nature. The passage to which he appeals in support of his views occurs in an appendix to the 'Lay Sermons'. The author is contemplating the perfection of the natural world, and his soul is moved to say to itself: 'From this state hast *thou* fallen! Such shouldst thou still become, thyself all permeable to a higher power'.

Mr Murry interprets this passage to mean that Coleridge was advancing a plea for 'the conscious achievement of a condition of pure spontaneity, in which state man should be so completely obedient to, and expressive of, Life as the rest of organic Nature appears to be'. He adds further:

> Thus we may describe Coleridge's philosophic poem as the supersession of intelligence, by intuition; of understanding, by reason. This process, achieved in the individual man, was redemption; by it man *became one with Nature,* for the spark of intuitive Reason is kindled in him by a contemplation of Nature . . . Nature *is* the Truth; and as man, by the attainment of Reason in himself, is reconciled with Nature, so he becomes part of the Truth—'all permeable to a higher power'. (*Things to Come,* p. 193)

Now all this, although it contains a great measure of truth, is really extremely misleading. Certainly it is plain to any person who reads the appendix carefully that Coleridge is attempting to describe the nature of a unified consciousness in which heart and head have become one. Certainly, also, it is true that by the attainment of Reason man is *reconciled* with Nature. But to be reconciled with

Nature is not the same thing as to be *one with* Nature, and it is perfectly clear that to present Coleridge as believing that man should, or could, do such a thing is a completely unjustifiable proceeding. The evidence against such a conclusion is, indeed, overwhelming.

Let us first of all consider the original passage from Coleridge in full, instead of breaking it off just at the point at which it ceases to support Mr Murry's conclusions:

> From this state hast *thou* fallen! Such shouldst thou still become, thy Self all permeable to a holier power! thy self at once hidden and glorified by its own transparency, as the accidental and dividuous in this quiet and harmonious object is subjected to the life and light of nature which shines in it, *even as the transmitted power, love, and wisdom, of God over all, fills and shines through nature*!

We may observe to begin with that (in all editions I have been able to trace) the words used by Coleridge were 'permeable to a *holier* power'. Mr Murry does not like the word 'holy'; it stands, indeed, for everything which he is most anxious to repudiate. His pen, therefore, writes instead the word 'higher'. Further, it is perfectly plain from Coleridge's words that what he meant to convey was that just as Nature is a medium for the expression, not, as Mr Murry would have it, of 'Life', but of *God*, so analogously should man also be an expression of God. In addition, between these two types of instrumentality—the manifestation of the Divine in man and the manifestation of the Divine in Nature—there is a profound affinity: to that which appears in man as Reason there corresponds in the objective realm the organic forms of Nature. But this correspondence is only explicable for Coleridge in terms of a theistic hypothesis. Two pages further on we find the passage:

> The fact, therefore, that the mind of man, in its own primary and constituent forms, represents the laws of nature,

is a mystery which of itself should suffice to make us religious: for it is a problem *of which God is the only solution*—God, the One before all, and of all, and through all!

It is, then, perfectly clear that Coleridge did not believe that man was 'one with Nature'. What he believed was that Man, Nature, and God existed in a threefold relationship: both Man and Nature reflect God's attributes, and it is only through their common dependence upon 'a holier power' that the processes of Nature can become intelligible to the human mind.

That Mr. Murry should attempt to adduce the authority of Coleridge in order to support his own naturalistic conclusions is certainly extraordinary. Not only the appendix from which he quotes, but the 'Lay Sermons' themselves and, indeed, the whole of Coleridge's works, are written from the standpoint of an extremely devout theist, a theist, moreover, whose demonstrations of the insufficiencies of a purely naturalistic philosophy are amongst the most subtle and powerful in modern criticism. A few paragraphs earlier in the same essay there occur the words:

> If you have accompanied me thus far, thoughtful reader, let me not weary you if I digress for a few moments to another book, likewise a revelation of God—the great book of His servant Nature. That in its obvious sense and literal interpretation, it declares the being and attributes of the Almighty Father, none but the *fool in heart* has ever dared gainsay.

The italics, I may say, are Coleridge's own.

5. 'Things as they Are'

I have now said enough, I hope, to show that Mr Murry's Naturalism presents several extremely unsatisfactory features. Even more serious are the problems raised by his attitude when we come to deal with its moral implications. As a preliminary to doing so we must consider his doctrine of the validity of 'things as they are', the purport of which will be sufficiently indicated by the following quotations:

For the secret of true religion . . . lies simply in the rediscovery of the actual—a rediscovery which can be fully accomplished only through a process of rebirth and reintegration. (*Things to Come*, p. 217)

The demand which the human soul makes is for satisfaction here and now; men's eyes must *see* their salvation. It is this visible salvation, if the phrase may be given, that great poetry does offer. It faces the real, it extenuates nothing, shrinks from nothing; it gives us life as it is. And we discover that we can desire nothing more perfect, for we can conceive nothing more perfect to desire. (*Ibid.,* p. 203)

What lies beneath the 'poetic' in all its infinite manifestations is an original awareness in the mind of him who created it that some fragment of experience was *valid*. . . . Not that it was significant *of* anything; it was significant of nothing but itself. Yet it was significant. And its significance appeared in its own sufficiency; it simply *was*. . . . We all have moments when . . . we suddenly find ourselves aware, so to speak, not of the existence of a thing, but of its being. It is just that thing, not an example of a class of things; we are aware of its manifest uniqueness. No thought of how it is, nor why it is, concerns us; it is abundantly sufficient *that* it is. (*New Adelphi,* II, iv, 326)

When we love a Fact, it becomes Truth; when we attain that detachment from our passions whereby it becomes possible for us to love all Facts, then we have reached our Peace. If a Truth cannot be loved, it is not Truth, but only Fact. But the Fact does not change, in order that it may become Truth; it is we who change. All Fact is beautiful; it is we who have to regain our innocence to see its Beauty. (*Studies in Keats,* 1930, p. 81)

That we are presented in these passages with a doctrine which makes a powerful appeal to our æsthetic sensibility it would be idle to deny. But at the same time we cannot but suspect that we have to do with one of those subtly plausible hypotheses which only disappoint us the more profoundly the more carefully we examine them. When the soft music has died away, the fumes of the incense have been dissipated, and the lights again raised, we find, as we have so often found before in similar circumstances, that our fatal suggestibility has once more led us astray.

Take first the conception which is implied of our relation to Reality. We are assured by Mr Murry that nothing can be more satisfying to us than a vision of things in their essence. Looked at with the eye of the poet, they appear as being completely 'valid'; we can ask for nothing more. Yet we *do* ask for something more. For the obstinate fact remains that if the beauty and goodness which we discern in objects are not derived from their participation in something which lies beyond themselves, then we are presented with a world of fugitive, everchanging elements the spectacle of which must finally become utterly oppressive to our minds. However wonderful things are 'in themselves', it remains true that we are precluded, in contemplating them, from establishing contact with anything more enduring than the Flux. The exquisitely beautiful apparitions which pass continually before our eyes do not become less ephemeral by reason of the fact that we have penetrated to their 'essence'; for that 'essence' involves nothing beyond themselves. An endless succession of lovely objects raises for us the same problem as an endless succession of commonplace ones. In each case we are limited to the realm of the phenomenal.

It is on such 'pure phenomena' on which Mr Murry would have us live. Not the 'pure (or primitive) phenomena' of Goethe, who regarded them as the ultimate expression of the invisible divine, but phenomena which represent the appearance of something as transient as themselves. And on such a basis man cannot live for long. However vehemently Mr Murry may assure us that 'supernatural religion is the refuge of those who cannot rest in things natural', one must insist that the whole weight of our deeper human experience is on the other side of the scale. The soul demands something more substantial than refined sensationalism. We find when we look within that we stand in relationship with Something that is enduring, Something that remains itself unmoved in the midst of the changing. And we have a deep and obstinate sense that that Changeless Something which we can thus internally realize is also in some inexplicable fashion behind the multifarious and shifting forms of the external world. A philosophy of pure æstheticism which leaves this realization out of account can never win our allegiance for more than a brief season. It may temporarily beguile the minds of those who have revolted from the abstractions of rationalism, but in the end it will leave us with dust and ashes in our mouths.

Again I cannot but feel that Mr Murry's conception of the fruits of illumination is singularly limited. We are informed that if we can only become 'reintegrated' we shall enjoy the privilege of seeing 'things as they are'. An apple, a baby, a landscape will become completely 'valid' for us, and we shall find that 'we can desire nothing more perfect'. I have no desire to minimize the significance of the contemplative experience. But it is necessary to point out that the consequences of mystical rebirth are usually considered as being of a very much wider character. The man does not simply perceive the 'validity' of the objects with which he is surrounded: he acquires certain very definite spiritual gifts, both of receiving and of giving. He becomes able to divine the working of the deeper processes of life: to heal, to bless, to master the occult forces of nature. Admittedly, there is a sense in which all these things are on a lower level than the experience of ecstatic vision. But it remains true that, in laying such weight upon the significance of contemplation, and leaving all the other fruits of emancipation out of account, Mr Murry is giving us a one-sided picture of the facts. There are other aspects of religion and they demand to be taken into consideration.

But the fundamental question raised by Mr Murry's pronouncements is that of the relation between the moral and the æsthetic elements in our experience. And here we must begin by enquiring how far this identification of Reality with something which lies altogether beyond the plane of the practical can be considered to be permissible. Mr Murry's attitude, it is to be remarked, is closely parallel to, and evidently influenced by, that of the French philosopher, M. Jules de Gaultier. In No. 2 of (what was then) his *New Adelphi* he printed, and at the same time commended to his readers, a translation of an article by this writer entitled 'The Limits of Intelligence and Faith', the core of which is to be found in the following passage:

> Religious sentiment, in its pure form of mysticism, recognizes morality as its sheer antipodes. Morality is the sense of the imperfection of existence. Mysticism is the sense of the perfection of existence. Morality desires to change that which is into something else, to transform evil into good. Mysticism desires to change nothing. It must sanctify with its approbation things-as-they-are. If the mystic makes a single move to change the wolf into a lamb, if he strives to dissuade the murderer from his crime, he has fallen from the rank of mystic, and, by showing that he believes it possible to change that which is, he betrays that he has exhausted, or that he never possessed, the power to sanctify and transfigure it. . . . The world in its totality, with no extenuation, cruel and revolting to our sensibility, outrageous to our reason, thus and not otherwise, such is the world which is lovely and good, such is the world which is perfection for the mystic, and if it is not this very world, with no extenua-

tion, that is vindicated through the mystic radiance, if a single cry of pain is suppressed, if a single crime is prevented, it is a sign that the grace of religion is inoperative and that the world is delivered over again to the sinister play of causality.

I have quoted this excerpt because it serves to bring out very clearly the type of distinction upon which M. de Gaultier, and Mr Murry after him, is working; the consequences which he draws from it will engage our attention later. The similarity of Mr Murry's attitude is indicated sufficiently by the following passage from an article by him published in the *New Criterion* (July, 1930):

> Religion, for the Naturalist, is precisely what remains when Ethics has been removed from Religion. . . . Because the Naturalist is not deluded into believing that his values or anybody else's have a transcendental sanction, he does not escape the necessity of pursuing this rather than that end in his own life. . . . Naturalism . . . replaces the hybrid combination of spirituality and morality, which is Religion, by a clean and perfect separation between them. It relegates morals to politics, and purifies spirituality to a quintessence.

Let us resist as far as possible the subtle influence of these writers' literary style and consider as dispassionately as we can the nature of the position to which they would commit us. They are affirming nothing less than that we cannot, by exercising the ethical will, enter in any way into the realm of Reality. Moral values have no 'transcendental sanction', for they pertain only to the plane of the relative; the spiritual lies completely beyond, to be apprehended only through the mode of 'contemplation'. Moral behaviour thus becomes a matter of physical inclination, of biological adaptation, without ultimate significance. The difference between true and false statements, between virtuous and vicious conduct, between beautiful and ugly music—these are not real, since every object can, provided one develops the appropriate consciousness, be equally 'sanctified' and 'transfigured'. We can enter into the realm of the spiritual by contemplating a stick or a stone which has miraculously become 'valid' for us, but not by living an honourable life or by suffering martyrdom for our beliefs.

The point to which I would first draw attention in considering this æsthetic philosophy is the attitude adopted by Mr Murry in putting it forward. The case is not laid before us with any completeness; we have, as usual, bare affirmation. No allusion is made to the fact that in following this particular path he is repudiating the conclusions of almost every philosopher who has concerned himself seriously with the problem of the implications of morality. As is well known, the corner-stone of Plato's system was the identification of the Real with the Good. Kant, again, believed that the truth of Religion was indisseverably connected with our consciousness of good and evil. In fact, it is difficult to name a single moral philosopher of repute who has not insisted that in the deepest roots of our moral being we are in some fashion involved in the Real. I am not asserting dogmatically that they were right in their conclusions; what I am doing is to protest against the unconcerned manner in which Mr Murry advances such subversive notions. There is no anxiety expressed at their extremely disturbing implications, no regret recorded that morality cannot somehow be *saved*: the contention that our values have no transcendental sanction is put forward without apology and without any apparent regard for the consequences to which it can lead. We cannot but feel that a greater measure of responsibility is demanded of a writer who is concerned with providing us with our spiritual values.

And now, to turn to the theory itself, we are beset with a doubt as to whether Mr Murry really means what he says. Does he mean that, when properly regarded, *all* facts are beautiful, or only that *some* facts are beautiful? Theoretically, of course, he is committed to the first view, but in practice, it would seem, he adopts rather the second.

What Mr Murry stands for in his most inspired moments is the 'romantic' attitude at its best. And the valuable element in that attitude is the consciousness which it awakens in us of the beauty and truth which lie hidden from all but the poet in the apparently commonplace objects and circumstances of life. Coleridge's famous passage regarding the capacity of genius to 'rescue the stalest and most admitted truths from the impotence caused by the very circumstance of their universal admission', affords a case in point. So also does Wordsworth's penetration to the deep humanity which lay beneath the humble exterior of the leech-gatherer. The strength of the true romantic lies in his sensitiveness to the 'wonder of the natural'. And it is, I believe, in assisting us to rediscover that wonder that Mr Murry is doing us his most characteristic service.

But it is another matter when he would have us conclude that to the purified vision *all* facts are beautiful. We are enjoined to 'browse, in contemplation, upon a baby or an apple tree'. Admirable advice to those who have been seduced by their intellectual faculties. But it is plain enough that such 'facts', even if their deeper import escapes the superficial eye, are in any case exceptionally agreeable to contemplate. Nor is the problem for us much more serious when we adjust our understandings to that of Keats. 'The poetic character . . . has as much delight in conceiving an Iago as an Imogen'. Here, again, it is evident that Iago is not simply a 'fact' taken at random, but essentially an attractive fact—for the sufficient reason that the Iago which is *conceived* (significant expression) is a very different being from the scoundrels who in real life provide the material for such an imaginative creation. Iago is, in fact, a scoundrel just in so far as the scoundrel has character, æsthetic appeal, and that beauty which attaches to the possession of a distinctive form. Nor does the principle apply any less even to such a creation as Joyce's Mr Bloom.

But if *all* facts can become truth for us if we regenerate our beings, how is it that the art which evokes for us a sense of the essential rightness of life is only able to achieve its object by presenting to us beautiful images? In the course of an essay on 'Poetry and Prayer' in *Things to Come,* Mr Murry has described to us in memorable language the regenerative power of great poetry. But the poem from which he quotes (Keats's *Ode on a Grecian Urn*) is woven throughout of lovely and graceful motifs; it does not directly present to us that life which, according to Mr Murry, it should induce us to 'accept'. Nor do I believe that, even in the case of such 'realistic' art as is capable of exercising this transmuting influence upon us, the artist is really able to produce his effects without withdrawing our attention in some subtle fashion from the ugly and commonplace features of that which is before us. 'The excellence of every art', wrote Keats, 'is in its intensity, capable of making all disagreeables evaporate from their being in close relationship with Beauty and Truth'. In other words, it is by virtue of the beautiful aspects of the object that the repulsive aspects are rendered acceptable to us. Does not this indicate decisively enough that even to the poet all facts are *not* beautiful?

What exactly does Mr Murry mean by 'things'? Does he not really mean any thing in so far as it exists in its natural, unperverted condition? Would he really be prepared to maintain that mutilated and imperfect forms are in themselves beautiful? That we can find a 'validity' in architecture which is grossly out of proportion, in half-starved animals, in vile typography, or in the features of a leper? I find it difficult to believe it.

Anyhow, whatever the force of these objections, the fact remains that for better or worse he has taken his stand on the uncompromising doctrine that 'all Fact is beautiful', and it is the consequences of this doctrine which we must now examine.

6. Æstheticism and Action

We may begin by glancing for a moment at a confusion which is implicit in the position adopted by M. de Gaultier. Returning to the passage quoted on a previous page, we find him advancing the view that the mystic who takes action has 'fallen' from his rank; he should be content to vindicate life 'through the mystic radiance'; the world must not be 'delivered over again to the sinister play of causality'. His concern is with perfection alone.

It should be apparent enough that this very intelligent critic has at this point failed to keep the issues clear. For he would have his mystic introduce into the time series something which is by definition beyond it, would have him in some impossible fashion live in two worlds at the same time. He must not 'strive to dissuade the murderer from his crime'. Yet it should surely be apparent that the fact that he finds himself confronted with a murderer at all proves he is in a situation in which the element of perfection cannot come into play. The encounter takes place on the plane of relativities; perfection lies beyond, in another dimension. Relative to that perfection, any action, good or bad, which takes place in the world of time is merely irrelevant.

The obligation upon the mystic is clearly to act. For inaction is as inappropriate to the plane of causality as action is to that of the changelessly real. The only answer to an action which takes place in time is some other action in time—not a withdrawal into another sphere, even if such a thing were possible. A burning house may from one point of view be something for us to 'vindicate through the mystic radiance', or 'sanctify with our approbation', but we are related to it also on the plane of the finite. And in this respect it is incumbent upon us to oppose the relative manifestation of fire with another relative manifestation—that of water. Indeed, the man who, confronted with the conflagration, would refuse to take any action with regard to it and treat it merely as an object for contemplation, is as impossible a figure as the philosopher who would decline to thank people for their kindness on the ground that all things are determined by the workings of immutable law.

The only consistent position for M. de Gaultier is to demand of his mystic that he should understand what he is doing, that he should not conclude that he is affecting Reality when, as he is humanly obliged to do, he is changing objects in the world. His error (if we adopt this particular philosophy) lies, not in acting wrongly, but in misinterpreting the nature of his deeds. Since all behaviour is spiritually meaningless, he may do what he likes.

Mr Murry's attitude is more logical. In an essay on 'The Philosophy of Poetry', he writes as follows:

If that which is possesses this perfection, then why struggle to achieve a better condition? This doubt often eats at the hearts of those religious souls who are in some degree responsive to the achievements of great poetry. It is the cause of that frequent revulsion in those who ponder the cause rather than experience the attitude of mind which often is called Pantheism. The great poet, no doubt, is a Pantheist, but he is primarily a poet. The Pantheism which, held as an intellectual creed, might engender a Stoic resignation is, as a poetic reality, a thing of potency—a *sursum corda*. For the poet's revelation of the perfection of what is kindles in our souls the desire to be able, with unaided vision, to see the perfection for ourselves. (*Things to Come,* p. 203)

Thus the important thing is that we should acquire the proper type of attitude to our experience. There is no question of aiming at an impossible compromise by sitting back with folded hands. As we have already seen, 'the Naturalist . . . does not escape the necessity of pursuing this rather than that end in his own life'. And this is sound enough. For if action has no relation to the plane of perfection, then we might just as well go on fulfilling our biological urges as not. Even though our behaviour has no transcendental significance, it is humanly satisfying and keeps us out of mischief. True, there is no really cogent answer to be made to the man who prefers to 'sanctify' the slums 'through the mystic radiance' rather than to undertake the unpleasant task of cleaning them up, but we must hope that his imagination will be touched by the further ideal which Mr Murry is laying before him of making himself a 'significant metabiological variation'. And, in any case, even if he does not so respond, it does not really matter, for, as we have already seen, there is no reason why the world should satisfy us 'save the desire of the human heart'.

Mr Murry does not pause to enquire whence this 'desire of the human heart' is derived. What I now want to urge is that it is associated in the most intimate fashion with our experience of 'perfection', and that in seeking to create a divorce between our moral impulse to action and our 'poetic' apprehension of the spiritual he is presenting the problem to us in a dangerously misleading light.

That there is a certain sense in which *omnis existentia est perfectio,* one is fully prepared to allow. Certainly art can, on occasion, awaken this feeling within us. And it would appear also that in their highest flights of mystical contemplation men have been vouchsafed a vision of a Reality which transcends all differences. Good and evil present themselves as purely relative terms; the soul perceives directly that 'all is Brahman'. This is a very lofty order of experience, and it is not to be dismissed by the more robust type of moralist as being merely illusory.

Yet certain difficulties remain. To begin with, we cannot help feeling that good and evil are not opposites in the sense that, say, male and female, or positive and negative, are opposites. Light does not simply complement darkness; it annihilates it. It is doubtful also whether the experience of that state of 'pure being' to which Mr Murry refers is not an experience of something essentially good, even though it may have taken up into itself that which we know as evil. Further, there must be some deep significance in the fact that the ecstasy which we derive from experiencing 'perfection' seems to be a more intense form of the joy which we derive from righteous behaviour—if, indeed, it is more intense. Again, for the majority of us the experience of acting morally is an experience of being involved deeply in the real. And, finally, we must give due weight to the fact that, however lofty the experience of 'perfection' may be, it is doubtful if it is more *certain* than our interior sense of the reality of moral obligation.

But we will leave these perplexing problems to those properly qualified to explore them. The point to which I now wish to draw attention is the more obvious one that, even if we concede that this vision of the absolute is authentic, we are compelled to recognize that it is so exceptional as to be of almost negligible significance. I have already questioned Mr Murry's assertion that *all* facts are beautiful to the true poet. The plain truth is that our æsthetic emotions are normally awakened as the result of contemplating those things which are harmonious, radiant, and pure. There may be a vision attainable for which an ulcerated limb or a heap of garbage is perfectly 'valid' and 'satisfying', but it is a vision which we can safely afford to leave out of account. The representatively human consciousness is the consciousness for which the spiritual is intimately associated with the good. The normal experience of man is that his sense of beauty is stirred by the sight of that which is the outcome of our efforts to give expression to the highest and noblest which we can conceive. And, even if we turn from human creations to Nature, we find that her beauty only reveals itself fully to the man who has disciplined his soul. For all practical purposes the spiritual may be said to appear only as the fruit of ethical striving.

A further consideration of importance. Whatever the nature of mystical vision, it remains true that it is *associated* with the moral in the most intimate possible fashion. Mr Murry has himself allowed that the apprehension of 'things as they are' is only to be enjoyed as the result of 'a process of rebirth and reintegration'. And this involves of a necessity intense *moral* effort. Hence one finds it a little misleading when he writes elsewhere (*God,* p. 124) that 'the mystical experience supervenes upon a state of complete spiritual exhaustion'. This evidently applies fully enough to the experience which he himself passed through early in 1923, and which is described in his *God*. But it would surely be more true to say of the normal mystical experience that, so far from supervening upon such a condition, it represents the final culmination of a state of intense spiritual vitality. As anyone may discover by referring to the authoritative works on the subject, the normal preparation for illumination is a long period of ascetic discipline. In the course of that discipline the spiritual energies are gradually intensified, until in a moment of supreme exaltation the man breaks through into a level which is beyond that upon which the consciousness is normally active. There may be a vision which follows upon the dark night of the soul, but it is not the only type that the mystic enjoys.

Nor is M. de Gaultier's account of the matter any more satisfactory. The 'essential activity' of mysticism, we learn, is 'to promote and develop in consciousness by peculiar means the certainty of this perfection'. But what are these 'peculiar means'? Certainly not some such subtle and deliberate twisting of the mind as this perverse sensationalist would seem to envisage, and which leaves the roots of the man unchanged. Nothing less, rather, than the complete transformation of the moral being, a transformation which, again, cannot be effectively accomplished without the persistent practice of virtue. Approaching the question from the other end, we may say that any type of alleged 'mystical vision' which cannot be eventually traced to the strenuous exercise of the ethical will must remain deeply suspect to our minds. The mark of the man who has attained to true illumination is that he will incidentally be conspicuous for his achievements on the plane of the moral.

And when we turn from the preparation for illumination to its consequences the association between the ethical and the spiritual presents itself to us with even more insistence. Hold, if you will, that the mystical vision relates us to the absolute: the fact remains that its outcome is an intense activity on the plane of the relative. This is the true 'mysticism of descent'. Whether or not the mystic has passed beyond the distinction between good and evil, his concern when he returns is plainly that of fostering one at the expense of the other. The sequence is, indeed, inescapable. For no man can enjoy a vision of the ultimate without being stirred to the depths of his being. And he cannot be so stirred without being impelled to give his emotion expression. And expression, again, is possible only on the level of the opposites. The experience of that which lies beyond all change leads inevitably to that ‘ changing of the world ’ to which M. de Gaultier would deny significance.

And here we are once more provided with a sure means for determining the authenticity of an alleged experience of illumination. We cannot follow the mystic on his lofty flights. But we are safe enough in concluding that if his vision is genuine it will impel him to unremitting moral effort. The fruit of an apprehension of ‘ things as they are ’ will be a determined attempt to change them, in so far as they are ugly and evil, into something else. Conversely, if we meet with a person who claims that he has contemplated ‘ perfection ’, and who is yet not living as a result upon a high ethical plane, we shall assume that, even if his experience was not altogether spurious, it was yet too fleeting and uncertain to be really worthy of the name.

In fine, what the mystical experience means for us in practice as individuals inhabiting a material and imperfect world is not poetry, but ethics. Our brief moments of ecstasy both presuppose, and commit us to, activity on the plane of morality. And in laying such inordinate stress upon the significance of that culminating instant when the spiritual is manifested with the breaking of the moral wave, Mr Murry must be held to be perverse. For he is presenting the cream of the experience to us without its implications, and thus falsifying the perspectives which open up before any person who is really concerned with the reintegration of his being.

7. The Mystic and the Poet

The theory, then, that we can enter into Reality more completely by the mode of contemplation than by the mode of action is seen to offer us difficulties of the most serious order. Since, however, the philosophy of pure æstheticism would appear to exercise—or at least to threaten to exercise—a peculiar spell upon the more sensitive minds of the present generation, I will venture to try the reader's patience somewhat further and explore the problem a little more deeply. And I will take as my point of departure Mr Murry's conception of the relation between poetry and mysticism.

That there is an intimate connexion between the experience of the poet and the experience of the mystic is a fact so obvious as scarcely to need stating. It has, moreover, an intimate bearing upon the problem of practical morality. How far can their respective experiences aid us in the task of rightly ordering our lives? Mr Murry has always been deeply conscious of the importance of this question, and he has discussed it with great care in his own writings.

As he sees the matter, the highest experience of the mystic and the highest experience of the poet can be regarded as being both complementary and equal in significance; they represent, in fact, a transcendence of the normal consciousness in two diametrically opposite directions:

> This contemplative experience appears to be the polar opposite of the mystical experience. Whereas the mystical experience essentially consists in the overcoming of the subject-object distinction, the contemplative experience essentially consists in carrying the subject-object distinction to perfection; it is the highest possible state of awareness of the object as object. This involves a diminution, even to the point of abeyance, of the perceiver's consciousness of himself as subject. (*New Adelphi,* I, ii, 107)

Further, he clearly recognizes (thus avoiding a misconception into which Mr Joad has fallen in his *Matter, Life, and Value*) that the true mystical experience, so far from being a sort of escape into a region of being from which nothing is brought back by the subject, is followed invariably by a fruitful outworking on the phenomenal plane of existence:

> In the complete mystical experience there are two phases or moments. There is the ascent into complete communion with the One, or with God, which is commonly supposed to be the end of the mystical path. It is not; the true and perfect mystic only ascends to the One in order to descend once more to the Many with the knowledge of its Oneness to sustain him. This is the doctrine of Plotinus and Dionysius the Areopagite and Meister Eckhart; but far more important even than these great masters of the mystical way, it is the doctrine of Jesus himself. Jesus was the most *perfect* mystic of whom we know. (*Things to Come,* pp. 215-6)

Mr Murry goes on to observe that 'the mysticism of descent can find its full expression in two ways alone: in life and in poetry'. Between these two ways there is, moreover, a close affinity, for 'a complete mysticism and a complete poetry are all but identical'. Yet with all this he advances the surprising proposition that 'the poetic experience is the perfection of the religious experience', and asserts that 'the mystic is but halfway to the perfect poet'.

What exactly Mr Murry here intends to convey is by no means clear. If a complete mysticism and a complete poetry are 'all but identical', why should the second be the perfection of the first? And why, again, does he say elsewhere of the poet that 'the interpenetration of the sensuous and the ideal, which he pursues as art, inevitably becomes an ideal of conduct and of life'? (*Things to Come*, p. 209) However, his general meaning does seem to be that poetry is in some sense the higher activity of the two. What attitude are we to take to this judgment?

Let me say at once that if Mr Murry is here thinking

of a type of mysticism which does not involve the element of 'descent', his view might be acceptable enough. But it would seem that he is not: he is speaking of the mystic who goes forth in action. And that such a man is in any sense living on a lower plane than the poet we simply cannot allow.

In any case, whatever may be Mr Murry's actual views on the question, it is a matter of some importance that we should examine it here. For I must again insist that it is very characteristic of the 'romantic' thinker, as, indeed, it is also of the more highly educated person today, to attach an altogether excessive significance to the æsthetic element in experience, and to show, on the other hand, a corresponding indifference to the possibilities of mystical living.

What we have to decide is whether a man will obtain a firmer grasp on reality by developing the mystical or by developing the poetic consciousness. And we can best approach the problem, I think, by observing that, whereas the mystic is primarily preoccupied with the subjective pole of experience, the poet is primarily preoccupied with the objective pole. That is to say, while one is principally concerned with *being* the other is principally concerned with *contemplation*.

Are we not here, at the very beginning, provided with a weighty reason for concluding that Mr Murry (if I have properly apprehended his meaning) has really inverted the truth? It is difficult not to allow that to embody reality is a more fundamental proceeding than to contemplate, however ecstatically, its embodiment in something outside oneself. The being of the poet is always tending to be dissipated, to be absorbed into the external world by which he is surrounded; the mystic, on the contrary, *becomes* the truth. Mr Murry has written that the poet is concerned with the Many rather than with the One. It would be equally true, and perhaps more illuminating, to say that he is concerned with the Not-self rather than with the Self. And it is just because, in his particular type of experience, the reality to which he is responding is outside the frontiers of his own being that his self-identification with it is *morally* less profound in its significance. Truth and goodness are not within him; they are reflected back to him from certain combinations of objects in the outer world. He does not possess the truth; he is exalted and harmonized as the result of projecting himself into it; he is polarized like a piece of steel in the neighbourhood of a magnet. And although he necessarily becomes to a degree that which he is contemplating, he becomes so only momentarily, by a reflex process of sympathetic association.

The principle is clear. A man is not truly mature while he still only apprehends truth and beauty at the cost of being conditioned by the objects in which they are manifested. If he falls into the error of drawing his vitality too extensively from a finite, material centre, he becomes lost when that centre is destroyed. For to derive one's sustenance from the world of concrete objects is, after all, to live by a reflected light. The soul is born into matter, which, to begin with, it naïvely takes to be something solid, enduring, and completely independent of the mind to which it appears. In childhood and adolescence we fail to distinguish between objects and the truth which they embody. The real is realized only in so far as it is incarnated in that which is before our eyes; when the object is removed we lose also all sense of that of which it was the vehicle. Goodness and beauty are as evanescent for us as is the rainbow which appears in the spray above the waterfall; when the water ceases to flow the rainbow also vanishes, and is as completely forgotten.

Gradually, however, as life advances, we become less dependent upon the phenomenal. The spiritual essence slowly acquires the greater reality and remains present to the mind whether it is actually manifested before our eyes or not. Forms are seen to be the expression of something to which we can hold fast whether they are preserved or not. We become less and less sustained by the physical embodiments of truth. We need less and less to reinforce our energies by contemplating Nature. The true and the good become real for us irrespective of the degree to which they find expression in material events. And this means a real emancipation. For in the phenomenal world they are manifested to different degrees, according to the fluctuations which occur in the struggle between the forces of darkness and light. The outer, visible universe is an ever-changing tissue of goodness and evil, of truth and falsehood, of beauty and ugliness, alternately elevating and depressing our spirits. But in so far as we can associate ourselves interiorly with the Real, we are raised above this plane of conflicting forces; for God everlastingly is, whether He shows his face to us or not.

Now this transfer of the source of spiritual vitality from outside to inside the soul signifies nothing else but a transition from the poetic to the moral plane. The poet's virtue lies in his impulse to embody the truth on the plane of art; he rightly abominates the word which has not been made flesh. But his creative strength is usually secured at the cost of a corresponding dependence upon the world of appearances. He tends to be *morally* weak—just because he has primarily identified himself with the Good through the medium of his senses. He is only too frequently at the mercy of that flux in which alone he is able to see the lineaments of reality reflected.

This is not to say that the finer type of artist is not a man of character; obviously, he must be if he is to be truly creative. In his *Civilized Man*, Mr McEachran has drawn attention to the fact that the pitiful servitude to 'temperament', which is, unfortunately, characteristic of the artist of today, may almost be regarded as a specifically modern phenomenon. But it will be admitted, I think, that the very fact that the artist is concerned so intimately with the seductive immediacies of sense renders it exceptionally difficult for him to achieve dispassionateness and serenity.

The strength of the mystic, on the contrary, lies in his power of realizing the Good subjectively. He finds it within himself. He becomes that which the poet contemplates. He is one with that which underlies the visible, and is therefore unaffected by the shadow-play of the world of appearances. He can pierce to the heart of the form without being conditioned by that form.

As a result, he is more firmly established in reality. The mystical and the contemplative experiences are not two equally significant opposites. In the psychological order the contemplative state comes first; the mystical state is only achieved afterwards by the process of gradually disentangling the real from that in which it appears. And it is a more fundamental state because, instead of the individual apprehending the unity of being as it is reflected in the forms of nature and the creations of art, he identifies himself with it interiorly by means of the *will*. As F. H. Bradley has written, 'although in science and art the real is realized, they are not religion, because the *conscious will* is not involved'. (*Ethical Studies*, 1927 ed., p. 321) Religious experience, in fact, just because it is essentially moral, is more *central*. It implies a union with the One of an infinitely more intimate and enduring type than that which is entailed in the contemplation of external reality.

It would be an easy matter to develop the theme further. The relative superficiality of the contemplative experience is sufficiently evidenced by the breakdown of the romantic attitude at the end of the average artist's life. In youth we are sustained for a season by æstheticism and ecstasy, but with advancing years there usually comes the discovery that, unless we can contrive to incarnate that which ravishes us from without, we are lost. The significance of that tremendous element in our experience, which was so powerfully stressed by Hebraism, acquires for us more and more force. Even if we are 'nature mystics' who are able to see Nature under the aspect of the divine, we yet find that we are not at rest until God is established within.

'The poet', writes Mr Fausset, 'is solving a problem, not merely of formal relations, but of his personal relation to the Universe'. This is from one point of view perfectly true. But the word 'solving' must be interpreted with care. Of most artists one may say that by a process of imaginative creation they both purge their being and resolve an intellectual or spiritual conflict within themselves. But the fruit of their struggle is more the attainment of vision than a profound reorganization of being. The man comes to *see* more clearly and expresses his newly found understanding in the form of a work of art. But although he is necessarily to some degree changed, it can hardly be said that he has actually *become* that which he has apprehended. He is a more perfect seer, but his problem is not fully 'solved'. That only happens when what he sees and what he *is* have become one.

And the proof of that identification is that he very frequently becomes dumb. For with most artists creation is incidental to a search for that condition of inner being in which the individual actually embodies the truth he contemplates. And, when that stage is reached, the urge towards artistic creation, *in so far as that creation is the expression of a striving towards the integration of the self*, is bound to die. There is no longer any impulse to deal with the problem in symbolical terms. For the artist does not, strictly speaking, express himself: he expresses that to which he is aspiring. And when he has become that which he previously only contemplated the function of art as a means for uniting the divided self becomes completely superseded. He may, indeed, continue to create, but he will do so from an entirely different motive: that of glorifying God.

8. The Word and the Flesh

So much for the general relationship between contemplating reality on the one hand and embodying it in one's person on the other. What I now wish to pass to is the closely related question of the comparative significance of expression in terms of art and expression in terms of being.

Since we are concerned with the positive movement of forthgoing involved in 'descent', we may leave the purely passive experience of contemplation out of account. Admittedly, there is a creative element in all appreciation, but it is scarcely possible to maintain that a man is 'expressing' himself when he is immobilized and entranced by art. The very fact that receptivity demands stillness and abstention from self-affirmation is a sufficient indication of the fact that the individual is submitting himself to an influence exercised upon him from without.

We will limit ourselves, therefore, to the problem of active expression. And we may observe to begin with that the actual creation of poetry, even if we use the term in the widest possible sense to include all forms of artistic creation, is the privilege of a talented minority alone. And what we are concerned with is the discovery of a way of life which is open to all. But in any case it is extremely doubtful whether the artist can be said to be creating in as vital and complete a fashion as the person who is expressing his identification with the One in terms of will.

Take first the actual process of artistic creation. One cannot fail to see that the artist's relationship with reality, although intimate, is not *immediate*. Although in the moment of creation he is 'expressing' beauty and truth, it cannot fairly be said that, even in this exalted phase, beauty and truth are *in* him. The degree of identification with reality is certainly greater than that which is entailed in the contemplative condition; it is more vital to paint a picture than to look at it. But the fact remains that, during the period in which he is creating, the artist is in a sonambulistic, trance-like condition. If in one sense he is intensely alert, he is alert only in order to direct with discretion that which is, so to speak, passing through his being. He is quite literally inspired, breathed into, momentarily possessed by a truth which is not primarily within him. And, when the intoxication passes, what he has 'created' often presents itself to him as alien and almost unintelligible. Any virtue which he possesses lies in the fact that he is sufficiently worthy to be a vehicle for inspiration, and though this means much it does not, as the records of the lives of so many artists go to show, signify the same thing as incarnating reality and expressing it through the will. The poet is a vessel, and notoriously a weak one.

There is also to be considered the fact that, although the artist expresses beauty and truth, he does not do so *directly*. He does not manifest reality immediately through his own person in the course of his association with his fellow-men, but only does so by employing certain arbitrary symbols. Art is artificial. If an artist uses his body—that which is nearest to his ego—to express himself, it is usually only in connexion with purposes which are set apart from the purposes of everyday life. He sings or mimes on particular occasions alone, on a stage and before an audience; he does not use his eyes, voice, or hands primarily to express reality in the course of his daily affairs. He *performs*—and a performance is essentially something symbolical and apart from the normal business of life. Or, again, the connexion between inner being and outer expression becomes still less immediate when, as a painter, he embodies his response to the beautiful in a canvas, as much as to say: 'If you want to know how the One manifests itself through me, look at *that*! There you will find the real me revealed'! And it is the same thing when a man refers us instead to a poem or a symphony—the embodiment is *outside* himself.*

The suggestion that, as a mode of expression, art creation is less central and fundamental than actually living out the truth, invariably awakens a deep antagonism in the mind of the typical sophisticated modern. For the notion that men and women could in their own beings embody reality with far greater completeness than it can be embodied in the forms of art has become altogether foreign to our understanding. Instead, we exalt the significance of art to an immoderate degree, forgetting that human personalities provide us with an infinitely more rich and plastic medium for the expression of truth and beauty than do pigments, words, or notes of music. No picture or poem can speak to the heart so powerfully and eloquently as the transfigured human being, and this for the reason that man is indeed the microcosm of the macrocosm, so that every force and potency which is active in Nature can find a vastly greater measure of expression through the physical body of man.

A poem, a picture, a piece of architecture—these are,

* I do not mean to suggest, of course, that there are not many artists who are so constituted that they are able to create in a more effective fashion on the plane of imagination than on the plane of life. But this does not alter the fact that the mode of expression which they have adopted is less vital from one point of view than that of the mystic.

after all, but forms upon which the spirit has left its signature. They have been crystallized into shape by the polarizing influence of a personality, but that personality is not still, as it were, *there* behind them; it has withdrawn to express itself anew through some other medium. All that we have before us is the rearrangement of matter which is the outcome of its activity. When, however, we are in the actual physical presence of the individual who has elected to express himself in terms of being, we can look through his eyes into the living soul. We are now separated from the self by the thinnest of the veils which can ever divide us from it. We meet with the spirit *in action*. The intellect, passion, and will, which might otherwise express themselves by impressing a significant form upon matter, now radiate upon us with direct and terrible power without any intervening medium between save that of the flesh. And the effect is infinitely more potent than that of anything which the individual has *done* or *made*. That which before we could only deduce from observing the creations of personality is there before us in its nakedness. The glance of the eye, the tones of the voice, the stance of the figure, reveal immediately that of which in terms of art we could only see the imperfect reflexion.*

Nor is this all. Not only could men and women in

* This would seem to be the logical conclusion of the argument advanced by Mr McEachran in his essay. He maintains therein that the noblest art is that which has the human as its subject-matter—a theory with which I would myself agree. But is not the next step that of recognizing that the subject-matter itself is still more fundamental than its reproduction? I do not mean that a picture of St Francis might not incidentally express something which could not be expressed by St Francis himself. But whatever St Francis did express directly by his personality certainly could not be so perfectly expressed by his portrait.

themselves become overpoweringly expressive instruments of reality, but it is open to them also to express reality in terms of their personal relationships. Proportion, symmetry, fitness for purpose—we are accustomed to look for these qualities first of all in the realm of art. But is it not evident that were we to become more completely spiritualized, the Good and the Beautiful would, through the operation of our perfected wills, be bodied forth, not only in forms distinct from ourselves, but in the very order of society? No symphony could be so magnificent as that which would be achieved when the component forces were within ourselves, when spiritual relationships, instead of being merely symbolized, were expressed in terms of our very being. *That which we were* would be itself a glorious tone poem, a poem which we did not simply passively listen to, but actually embodied. The harmonies which charmed our ears, the proportions which ravished the eye, would be expressed in terms of living units, would be actually incarnated. Being and contemplation would become one—or at least far more perfectly reconciled than in any other possible mode.

I do not mean, of course, that a perfected humanity would have no use for the arts. On the contrary, out of the exuberance of their being they would be impelled to express truth, not only in action, but by the creation of forms of art. But, as I have already suggested, such secondary and less immediate expression would represent, as it were, the overflowing of something which was already harmonized in itself. It would constitute a more extended manifestation of that which was already established within the being; it would not be incidental to the struggle to attain to it. The art of such an epoch would be the serene art which comes after reintegration and not that agonized self-exploration which precedes it.

To enlarge further upon the difference between the immediate and the less immediate expression of reality would be out of place here. All I wish to bring out is the fact that our primary aim must necessarily be that of achieving the first, and the more fundamental, of the two. And where writers like Mr Murry lead us astray is by placing the emphasis on the wrong point and refusing to recognize with any completeness, not only that personality and human relationships constitute the most perfect available medium for the expression of reality, but that it is this type of expression which we should be most concerned to achieve.

Not that Mr Murry has not written many admirable pages on the theme of rendering oneself an expressive instrument for Life. But he has confused the issues by asserting elsewhere that the poet is higher than the mystic. And this, as I hope I have made clear, is an altogether unacceptable conclusion.

9. Contemplation and Catharsis

We are obliged, then, to conclude that the most significant possible expression of beauty and truth is that which is accomplished, not in terms of art, but in terms of being. What we must now consider is the degree to which art can aid us in transmuting our basic natures.

To achieve any real measure of psychological stability is an undertaking of the utmost difficulty. The resistance of the mass of men and women to suggestion is painfully low. They tend to be swayed by every passing attraction, to be enslaved by their own vanities and ambitions, to become enmeshed in the net of their unregenerated passions and desires. This is a fact, a fact which no truly realistic thinker can afford to ignore. Nor, as one would expect, has Mr Murry failed to perceive its significance. In a remarkable essay on 'The Need for a New Psychology' he has, indeed, frankly expressed himself as appalled by the problem which confronts the reformer of providing men with a means for resisting the temptations with which they are assailed in our present-day world.

Man is pitifully weak. How is he to be spiritually strengthened? The humanitarian, as we have seen, places his trust to a large degree in the influence of environment. The classical humanist relies upon a type of intellectualistic philosophy which we have found reason to reject. What has the romantic to offer us instead?

The aim which he would set before us is that of expressing in terms of life the same consciousness which the poet expresses in terms of art. We must live as artists, or, as Mr Fausset has expressed it in his *Modern Dilemma*, we must live by the light of Imaginative Reason:

> We must subordinate both our rationalism and our ethics to æsthetic imagination. Or, in simpler words, we must approach life in all its multitudes of aspects as an art demanding the same patience, the same sensitiveness, the same discipline, the same resolute self-forgetfulness and self-knowledge, the same passion for truth, as the art of poetry.

The parallel is suggestive enough. But it is important that we should take due account of the fact that the capacity to create on the poetic level does not necessarily bring with it any notable ability to create on the level of life. In fact, it would often seem to represent a compensation for a failure to do so. For, as Mr Fausset points out:

> The association of distracted lives with great poetry, when it has occurred (and it has occurred far less often than is popularly supposed), is due to the fact that the poet has been driven the more desperately to resolve in his art the discords which tortured him in his life.

And we find Mr Murry making a very similar observation:

> Poetry exists chiefly in a state of imperfection: for the most part the harmony in the soul of the poet out of which

it is created, and the harmony in the soul of the reader which it creates, are alike momentary and evanescent. There seems, indeed, no link between this glimpse of the divine and men's actions in the world: nor is there generally more than a precarious connection between what a poet is and what he utters. (*Things to Come,* p. 207)

This is a sober enough comment. On the next page, however, we find him writing in the following strain:

In order that we should understand what the poet is saying, we also need to be changed, to be reborn. And poetry in this its highest form has *direct* power: its spiritual significance is so concentrated that it acts upon the receptive soul as that leaven which 'a woman took and hid in three measures of meal'. Poetry at its highest does not *mean* anything, it *is*; it cannot be understood, it can only be received; it is a pure conduit of mysterious and ineffable life into man's being. He, too, becomes touched with significance.

This is beautifully enough expressed. But we cannot forget that Mr Murry has just admitted, with Mr Fausset, that neither the writing nor the reading of poetry has the effect of transmuting the being in any fundamental or enduring sense. The situation remains substantially unchanged.

The truth is that Mr Murry is here finding himself confronted with a fact which he is at heart extremely unwilling to face: the fact that the basis of character is *moral.* Wherever possible, he attempts either to disregard or to slur over it. Take this again:

The complete interpenetration of the ideal and the sensuous, after which the poet unconsciously strives as the highest poetic excellence, intuitively perceived, serves, in the man of supreme genius, as an earnest of a condition to be achieved within himself. The interpenetration of the sensuous and ideal, which he pursues as art, inevitably becomes an ideal of conduct and of life. So through a loyal obedience to the poetic noêsis the full perfection of religious noêsis—the Word made flesh—is reachieved. (*Ibid.*, p. 209)

It is not, I hope, out of place to point out that a vision of an ideal and the attainment of that ideal are not exactly the same thing. What at the beginning of the paragraph appears as 'an earnest of a condition to be achieved' becomes by the end of it, under the influence of Mr Murry's style, something which has actually been accomplished: 'The full perfection of religious noêsis—the Word made flesh—is reachieved'.

No less revealing is the following passage:

> But it (Poetry) does lucidly and unforgettably whisper: 'This thou shalt *be*'. Valid experience is such that, once we have glimpsed it as possibility, we are wholly turned towards making it a reality. A profound and secret discipline is imposed upon us. (*New Adelphi*, II, iv, 328)

I may be doing Mr Murry an injustice, but I must confess that the effect of such pronouncements upon me is to suggest forcibly that he is attempting to evade the real issue by the process of fusing together the vision of the ideal and that which is implied in attaining to it. If we yield ourselves unguardedly to the subtle influence of his extraordinarily accomplished style, we find ourselves sooner or later infected with the belief that in submitting ourselves without reserve to poetry we are already more than halfway to realizing that religious 'noêsis' which it inspires us to achieve. The atmosphere is, in fact, dangerously 'romantic'; one suspects that Mr Murry is trying to sweep us over obstacles which in reality are not so easily to be surmounted.

'A profound and secret discipline is imposed upon us'. What does that discipline entail? Not only an active attitude of mind instead of that passive attitude which is implied in yielding oneself to the influence of poetry, but also, one must insist, preoccupation with an altogether different type of experience. Certainly no intelligent person will deny that Poetry, besides presenting us with ideals, can also furnish us with spiritual refreshment. But no truly realistic thinker will fail to recognize that the real labour of transmuting the lower nature involves a concern with a very definitely *un*romantic aspect of existence. To pass from expressing the One in terms of imagination to expressing the One in terms of personality is to find oneself in a different realm of being. What we become committed to as a result is asceticism. And in so far as we practise asceticism we turn our backs—for the time being, anyway—on poetry and romance.

I shall develop the point at some length in bringing this chapter to a conclusion. But before leaving the subject I must say a further word regarding Mr Murry's attitude to the poetic. The emphasis which he lays upon the regenerative function of Literature generally, and of Poetry in particular, strikes me as being almost fantastically exaggerated. 'Literature is become the great religious adventure of the human soul'. (In *The Necessity of Art*, p. 165) 'Any declaration of the quality of God, or of anything else in earth or heaven, that is to be compulsive and creative, must be made by means of poetry'. (*New Adelphi*, II, iv, 323) And so on. But it is only necessary to reflect for a moment, on the one hand upon the wide range of human psychological types, and on the other upon the variety of experiences which are offered us in the universe, to perceive how hopelessly one-sided such a view of the matter must be.

Life is educative at every point. Men learn their lessons from their daily association with others, from submitting themselves to authority, from listening to the voice of their direct inspiration, from sport and play, from religious observances, from mastering the forces of nature—in fact, by means so various that it is out of the question to enumerate them. And it is further a matter of commonplace observation that no one of these educative agencies can legitimately be exalted above any other. It is possible to read good literature with discernment and yet remain disintegrated, because the more important lessons presented by the immediate environment have never been properly faced. And it is possible also to dispense altogether with the works of Chekhov, Hardy, Keats, and Mr Murry's other heroes, and yet become firmly established on a basis of reality. To assume without question that the supreme means of enlightenment provided for mankind on this planet is that of reading books is to lose all human perspectives.

The truth is that the whole of Mr Murry's thinking on these problems is conditioned to an unfortunate degree by the character of his personal sympathies. 'I regard myself', he has written, 'primarily as a literary critic who has been forced by circumstances, both private and professional, to wander for a season in the debatable land wherein literature and religion find their culmination'. (*Things to Come*, p. 86) The consequence of this particular approach to the subject is a palpably exaggerated estimate of the function of literature as a spiritualizing agency. For a minority poetry is indeed the 'guide of life', and, in so far as Mr Murry is engaged in interpreting its message to us, we cannot be sufficiently grateful for his services. But his indifference to the manifold other ways in which men can realize the spiritual strikes me as positively disastrous—disastrous at least in the case of one who takes upon himself the responsibility of offering his fellow-men a practical philosophy of life. He lacks, in fact, the first qualification for such an office—a sense of proportion. It is not, indeed, too much to say with Mr T. S. Eliot that 'for Mr Murry poetry—or at least that poetry that he likes—is a substitute for everything; not only for the "abstract conceptual thinking" of science and philosophy, but for religion itself'.

The comment is perfectly justifiable. For we find that he does not merely overstress the significance of Poetry: he presents us also with a system of philosophy which denies to us the possibility of seeking satisfaction from any other quarter. The consolations of Religion are withheld from us, since it has been established that God does not exist. Action, we are assured, is a mode of expression which is altogether inferior to that of poetic contemplation. And Reason can take us only but a short distance, since Mind, as he conceives the matter, is impotent to lay hold on Reality. It would seem, in fact, that it is Keats and Shakespeare or nothing.

10. The Background of Beauty

I have now examined all the more important issues which are raised for us by Mr Murry's philosophy. It remains, in bringing this chapter to a conclusion, to make some attempt to determine the extent of our debt to the New Romanticism.

That the strength of the romantic lies in his exceptionally clear and complete vision of that which belongs to the order of perfection will be evident enough. His preoccupation is with the spiritual. And the spiritual only finds a true expression at that point at which the ideal and the sensuous have become one. Reality is only fully revealed when the spiritual at once transmutes, and is conditioned by, the material. It is only the incarnated word which is truly compulsive.

Nor is it less apparent that the romantic's peculiar sensitiveness to the character of accomplished perfection is reflected with great faithfulness in the attitude which he adopts towards the problem of morality. One cannot but observe that both Mr Murry and Mr Fausset, for instance, are before everything concerned with that final flowering of personality which is the fruit of the integration of the divided self. Before their eyes is the image of the New Man who has again become reconciled with Nature. And they thereby, as I have already suggested, attain to a far more profound conception of the implications of spiritual regeneration than do such thinkers as Mr Babbitt, who are content to leave us in the end with an unresolved dualism on our hands.

This capacity to evoke for us a vision of the ideal is manifestly of immense value. We cannot achieve any real progress until we have acquired a proper comprehension of the final goal of our endeavours. And here the romantic can enlighten and inspire us as can no one else. Yet at the same time we are reluctantly forced to conclude that his attitude is in its own way as one-sided as that of the classical humanist with whom he finds himself in dispute. For although he has a clearer understanding of the ultimate aim to be achieved, he betrays an imperfect realization of what is entailed in the process of attaining to it. His gaze is directed to the statue; he tends to pay insufficient regard to the pedestal which serves it as a foundation.

Our modern romantics have realized very clearly that the corollary to the contemplation of the spiritual as it is manifested without must be the creation of the New Man within: 'This thou shalt *be*'. In other words, we must turn our attention from poetry, which is the expression of reality on the plane of imagination, to practical mysticism, which is the expression of reality on the plane of life. The point which I now wish to stress is that this enterprise can only involve a preoccupation with that region of experience in which the romantic is least at home. For that liberation for which he is striving can only be won at the cost of developing, to begin with, certain specifically 'classical' virtues.

The life of the spirit has two great complementary aspects: that of inward realization and that of outward expression. If either that realization or that expression is defective, we are concerned with an imperfect adaptation to life. The man whose strength lies in the phase of expression is the romantic; he is endowed with a feminine sensitiveness to the richness and intricacy of the realm of sensuous experience. But, as we have seen, he is on that account peculiarly exposed to the danger of being overpowered by the matter which he is seeking to spiritualize. The man whose strength lies in inward realization, on the other hand, is the classicist and, on a higher plane, the man of religion. He may have a notably inferior capacity for relating the temporal to the eternal, but he is remarkable for his moral depth and stability of character. He is massive and consolidated where the artist is fragile and inconsequent. In fine, while one type is particularly sensitive to the Changing, the other is particularly sensitive to the Changeless. One possesses the capacity to spiritualize the fugitive, the other the capacity to reflect in his personality the stillness and peace which is to be found at the heart of reality. The strength of one finds expression in relation to the Not-self, the strength of the other in relation to the Self. Both are by themselves incomplete. Only when they are united in the person of the true mystic is perfection achïeved. For just as the accomplished poet effects the union of the eternal and the temporal on the plane of art, so does the true mystic effect the same union on the plane of life.

What I would urge is that our romantics fail to give due recognition to the fact that the New Man must be as securely related to the changeless world within as to the changing world without. Their attitude in respect to this matter is definitely naturalistic and on that account unsatisfying.

Consider first of all their conception of the relation of the 'reintegrated' individual to the world of organic life. He has been reborn. The dualism of the divided self has been overcome. But can he, strictly speaking, be said to be 'reconciled' with Nature? And if so, in what sense?

It is one of the cardinal tenets of Mr Murry's faith that the highest which we know within us is purely natural in its origin. His use of the term 'metabiological' must not here lead us astray:

> Metabiology is biology into which what are known as 'values' are organically incorporated. . . . The process (of manifesting 'true creative newness') is strictly biological, but it cannot be contained in the category of the biological as it is used today. . . . We call it a metabiological variation because Biology is at present unable to recognize it. (*God*, pp. 182, 187, 209)

Nor is the attitude of Mr Fausset widely different. A study of the crucial passages in his *Proving of Psyche* leads one to conclude that in the regenerated man the life of Nature has, as it were, flowered into self-consciousness. There is no discontinuity involved; we are concerned with a straightforward process of evolution:

> The primitive force, which sustains the life of Nature, has blended in them with the moral values and the rational discrimination which belongs to man. . . . For man cannot reason aright until his mind obeys, while it informs with human meaning, the vital impulses which he shares as an instinctive being with all organic life. . . . He has, in short, to co-operate as a conscious being with the unconscious will of Nature.

Any approach to this difficult question must be tentative. But we are faced with the fact that man's actual experience of the workings of this new life within him suggests very strongly that, so far from being Nature raised to a higher power, it is actually *contrary* to Nature. We feel, indeed, that Mr Fausset is nearer the mark when he writes that 'only in fact when he is himself truly moral, by being truly creative as Jesus was, does he perceive that the purpose and processes of physical life *correspond* with those which govern his own activity'.

May it not be more true to say of the New Man that he has actually faced about, that he is now, as it were, experiencing everything all over again from the other end? That the wheel has turned full circle, so that he finally comes to rest exactly *opposite* Nature—so exactly that he is able to spiritualize her forms and master her forces? It cannot escape our attention that the condition of dualistic tension which precedes liberation involves a determined resistance to Nature. This we are obliged to admit. Any attempt to represent the experience of 'conscience' as a purely intra-biological conflict, of the same order as that which takes place between competing instincts, is surely doomed to failure. Our immediate experience—and it is our immediate experience which must in the end be the decisive factor—is that of something which is different from, and hostile to, the natural asserting itself against our impulses. And if we once concede this fact we shall find it difficult to believe that the outcome of the conflict can leave us still on the plane of the natural. The very term 'rebirth' implies that the old order has been transcended.

But I will not pursue this difficult subject further here. Let me turn instead to the romantic's attitude towards the problem of bringing this 'new man' into being. And here, I think, the manner in which he is limited by his naturalistic sympathies will be more clearly evident. The aim which he has set before himself is that of becoming a practical mystic. And this, as we have seen, entails a preliminary repudiation of the Changing and a concern instead with the Changeless. But the obligation discovers the romantic at his weakest point. For his intense responsiveness to the natural brings with it inevitably a marked dependence upon his physical senses. As soon as he can no longer bring them into play in relating himself to reality he loses his assurance and authority. He is supreme in apprehending the divine when it has found expression without, but correspondingly uncertain in apprehending the divine within. The invisible, the unmanifested, the incorporeal defeat him. His concern is with the flower and not with the seed out of which it has grown. His experience is excessively Hellenistic, insufficiently Hebraic.

The attitude of Mr Murry is in this respect typical enough. We are met on the one hand with a superb power of poetical evocation, an exquisite responsiveness to the ideal, a sure grasp on everything which pertains to the order of expressed perfection—the romantic vision, in fact, at its highest and its most intense. But we find that when there is no longer any sensuous element involved in the process of comprehending truth, when he becomes concerned with the more interior aspects of experience, his power seriously weakens. His almost cynical treatment of the problem of 'conscience', his limited conception of the moral order prevailing in the universe, his undiscerning attitude towards men's testimony to an interior experience of God, his unyielding naturalism, his extreme teachings regarding the nature of 'things as they are'—all this points only too decisively to the fact that we have to do with a thinker who, although he has a deep understanding of some of the most profoundly mystical elements in our experience, is yet too palpably conditioned by his physical senses to be properly qualified to lead us out of the perplexities in which we have become involved.

Our final conclusion, therefore, must be that the romantic who is committed to the enterprise of expressing reality in terms of life will have to learn to look at such conceptions as that of the 'inner check' with a more sympathetic eye. It is true that the classicist fails to realize that the fruit of the exercise of that ' check ' should be a transcendence of the plane of morality altogether. But it is true also that the romantic usually does not perceive that the synthesis of head and heart after which he is striving is to be accomplished only as a result of a concern with certain definitely unpoetic aspects of experience. For the Self within is only to be created and consolidated by a discipline which involves a deliberate turning away from the world of the senses. The basis of the romantic virtues is provided, in fact, by the virtues of the classicist.

The fact must be faced that the transition from poetry to mysticism, so far from representing a process of extension along the same horizontal plane, involves, rather, concern with an absolutely different dimension of experience. Between the within and the without there is a definite opposition. The poet has little to learn regarding the possibilities of the natural world. But if he turns from contemplation to being he is confronted with the task of creating within himself that motionless and impassive centre from which alone he can safely venture forth to transform it. He must become familiar with that inner world of being which reveals itself to the soul only when the senses have been stilled. To associate himself with the Changeless indirectly by contemplating it as it irradiates and transfigures the corporeal is no longer enough: he must make a resolute act of introversion and realize it anew as the immutable Self within. He must balance his native responsiveness to the differentiated by an inward association with that out of which differentiation comes.

Further, to achieve any progress along this interior path the would-be mystic, no less than the adept in the art of expression, must have recourse to a very definite technique. The Self within is not to be realized, save in the most intermittent fashion, without the exercise of a certain type of spiritual discipline—that discipline which makes, not for responsiveness to life, but for that inner serenity which is enjoyed by the saint and which the artist so rarely knows.

To discuss the possibilities which are open to the seeker in this particular direction is outside the scope of this essay. But it is not out of place to recall the fact that the most effective spiritual disciplines are those which centre upon a central Object which at once inspires the individual with humility and serves for him as a sustaining source of inspiration and power. All religious exercises which fail to bring one into relationship with such a Centre are on the same plane only as dietetics or eurhythmics—valuable, but with no capacity to affect the deeper levels of the being.

Can the romantic, any more than the classicist, really solve his problems without such a point of focus for his aspirations and energies? Will a World Organism, a Realm of Spirit, or a Sense of the Whole serve the same purpose? Can he, as Mr Murry would have him do, build the same type of arch as that built by the theist and yet consolidate it with an altogether different kind of keystone? Can he gain sufficient inspiration for the spiritual life by clinging to the idea of making himself into a 'significant variation', or an adequate 'instrument of life'? Manifestly the matter is not one for argument. As to whether or not men can live by such ideals the future will surely show. My concern throughout this book has been that of laying before the reader as fairly as I can certain aspects of the problem which we are today prone to leave out of account in discussing it.

APPENDIX

I MAKE no claim in this essay to have undertaken anything like a complete review of the literature bearing upon modern Humanism, with which indeed it is scarcely possible to keep pace. But it would be inexcusable to omit all reference to a remarkable work, *The Ascent of Humanity* by Gerald Heard, which was published in 1929, and has only recently come to my notice. The significance of Mr Heard's study in relation to our present enquiry lies in the fact that he has independently arrived at strikingly similar conclusions to those advanced by Mr Fausset in his *Proving of Psyche* (published actually in the same year) and by myself in these pages. For his fundamental assumption is that the soul which was originally unconsciously at one with Nature, and which then with the growth of self-awareness became divided, egocentric and devitalized, can only become whole again by attaining to a new unity in the One. Our basic problem in fact is that of transcending individualism and passing thereby altogether beyond the 'humanistic' plane. The New Man must be born, but he can only come into being as the result of a profound modification of consciousness.*

But whereas the New Romantics have arrived at their convictions as the outcome of a poetic type of experience, and whereas I myself have approached the question from

* I should add that the theory that the evolution of consciousness passes through these three stages was actually put forward in a very definite fashion by the late Edward Carpenter in his *Pagan and Christian Creeds,* first published in 1920. But neither Mr Fausset nor Mr Heard appears to owe him any substantial obligations. I myself only first learned of the anticipation through a reference to Carpenter in a remarkable article by Mr D. L. Murray entitled 'Is a New Religion Emerging?', published in *The Aryan Path* for July 1930.

the angle of religion, Mr Heard has been led to his conclusions by following the path of strictly scientific investigation. Where we appeal to introspection he comes forward with a powerful demonstration of the inevitability of this new attitude to the world. He shows, by a singularly discerning and exhaustive analysis of the course of past history, that the evolution of mind is in the direction of the emergence of 'super-individual consciousness'.

I am well enough aware that the educated are inclined, quite rightly, to regard all philosophies of history with deep suspicion. And the attitude is fully justified. But I doubt whether any imaginative person can read through Mr Heard's book and not be driven to admit that he has made out an impressive case for the view that the key to the nature of the modern epoch lies in a radical change in human psychology, a change which has up to the present—just because it has not yet proceeded far enough—been almost completely misinterpreted even by the most intelligent minds. We are entering upon a phase of consciousness which is altogether new, and it is only on the basis of this assumption that the otherwise bewildering manifestations with which we are today surrounded can become comprehensible to us.

All this is not to say that I am in unqualified agreement with this author's views. His interpretation of the religious experience, for instance, strikes me as unsatisfactory. And I feel that the historical sweep of the process which he envisages—'from group consciousness through individuality to super-consciousness'—is far too narrowly conceived. But I wish to stress, not these differences, but the extraordinary concurrence of opinion referred to above. In this concurrence there is surely something to cause even the most rationalistic thinker to pause and reflect.

INDEX